Contents

GREAT WOMEN OF ACHIEVEMENT

Women Inventors Who Changed the World

Sandra Braun

rosen publishing's
rosen central®
NEW YORK

For Maurine

This edition first published in 2012 by:

The Rosen Publishing Group, Inc.
29 East 21st Street
New York, NY 10010

Library of Congress Cataloging-in-Publication Data

Braun, Sandra.
Women inventors who changed the world/Sandra Braun.
p. cm.—(Great women of achievement)
"First published by Second Story Press, Canada, 2007"—T.p. verso.
Includes bibliographical references and index.
ISBN 978-1-4488-5996-2 (library binding)
1. Women inventors—Biography—Juvenile literature.
2. Women—Biography—Juvenile literature. 3. Inventions—History—Juvenile literature. 4. Technological innovations—History—Juvenile literature. 5. Social change—History—Juvenile literature. I. Title.
T39.B73 2012
609.2'52—dc23

2011032731

Manufactured in the United States of America

CPSIA Compliance Information: Batch #W12YA. For further information, contact Rosen Publishing, New York, New York, at 1-800-237-9932.

Christine Hobberlin, Editor

Introduction

They say that necessity is the mother of invention, that we are driven to create things when we need something that doesn't yet exist. Almost everything we use in our daily lives—the medicines we take to feel healthy, the appliances or gadgets we use in our homes for convenience or entertainment, or the technology we use in school or at work—started out as a single idea of one person.

While researching the lives of these impressive inventors, I felt humbled. They are all big thinkers and problem solvers—the type of people who can see a need for something that does not yet exist and can imagine how to make it happen, all the while believing that they will succeed.

It's one thing to have an idea for an invention, but quite another to follow through and make your idea a reality. All of the women in this book grew up in very different surroundings and circumstances. Some came from large families, were surrounded by loving and supportive people, and had the education and money to help them along. Some had to struggle through hardships without many of the opportunities others were given, yet they all shared a sense of determination and a faith in themselves and their ideas that drove them to success.

They had to have that drive and faith. Inventing is hard work. There are many steps to inventing besides having an idea. Most of the time, you have to make many different designs, called prototypes, and test them out to find out what works and what doesn't—and why. Once the design is perfected, the inventor has to patent her idea to make sure no one else can use the same idea to make another product. Next, the inventor has to find a way to make all the products she has to sell. In the beginning, before enough people know about the invention to make it a success, the inventor usually has to have another job as well. This can mean working all day at one job and then coming home to work all night on the invention. Usually, word of a good invention will travel quickly. At a certain point, an inventor will have to put together a plan for manufacturing, marketing, and selling her product to a wider audience. She has to go from being an inventor to being a businesswoman.

You can see why, with all of these jobs to do, inventors have to be dedicated and believe in themselves. There are no courses that teach you how to become an inventor, no handbook that can give you all the answers you need to make sure that every single thing works out as you planned every step of the way. Inventing is a process of trial and error, and of discovery. None of the women in this book was discouraged when her ideas took time and effort to be perfected. As Wendy Murphy, the inventor of a hospital stretcher built especially for infants, says, "There is no such thing as failure; every step in the process is a learning experience and helps you on your way toward your goals."

Some inventions—like Laurie Tandrup's Travelbud—begin as a solution to a personal short-term problem; but it's hard to keep a good idea secret for long! Laurie was stuck without a proper car seat for her son and needed to make something that would help her out of a jam. When it turned out that other people could use it too, the invention took on a higher purpose and now is used in hospitals to help many fragile newborn infants. C.J. Walker mixed up a hair treatment to help improve her own health and appearance. Little did she know that her cream would benefit her in many other ways and give jobs to thousands of women across the country, too.

Other inventions are born out of the inventor's desire to help all people. When Gertrude Elion made the decision to become a cancer researcher, she did not do it to solve her own problems, but to help other people get better and stay healthy. The drugs she created during her long career did just that. Sultry actress Hedy Lamarr designed her secret communication system to help her new country fight in World War II.

Sometimes, an invention improves on something that already exists. Patricia Bath's invention didn't create the practice of eye surgery, but changed it for the better. Stephanie Kwolek was seeking to create a new generation of synthetic fibers that would be stiffer, stronger, lighter, and more durable than anything previously invented by humans or nature. The result was Kevlar, which is now used in tires, brake pads, fiberoptic cables, the shells of spacecraft, suspension bridge cables, ski equipment, camping gear, canoes, parachutes, safety helmets, bullet-proof vests, and body armor. Inventions can also include the discovery of something that already exists in nature. Lise Meitner didn't create nuclear fission, but no one ever knew it existed before her experiments. She proved that it was real, described it for others, and gave it a name that people could recognize.

Finally, some inventors create new things to serve the work that they do. Lillian Gilbreth spent her whole life trying to find new ways to do work in offices, factories, and at home. Though it wasn't her original goal to be an inventor, she made many new products, like a garbage can with a foot pedal, which helped make her work and home environments more efficient. Bette Nesmith Graham, a secretary at the time, made Liquid Paper to help her correct the mistakes she made while typing. Engineer Elizabeth MacGill created innovative designs throughout her career and designed planes for the British during World War II.

We are all inventors. Every day, we each find small ways to make our own lives better or easier, by thinking of new ways to do things or creating makeshift solutions to overcome the problems we face. The difference is that these women took their ideas and made them into something that other people could use too. This is what intrigued me the most. I wondered why these women were inspired to invent and what drove them to make their ideas real.

As you look at the things around you now, at home and at school, I hope you think a little bit about how they were created. Each one came from the imagination of an observant, insightful person who saw a need and worked very hard to fill it. And I hope that you too will begin to think of how to make your life, and the lives of other people, better by using your own imagination and becoming a problem solver.

— Sandra Braun

Chapter 1

Madam C.J. Walker

(Sarah Breedlove) 1867–1919

When Sarah Breedlove was growing up, she did not have much—not the freedom to go where she wanted and do what she pleased, not the opportunity to go to school, and not the money to eat healthy food or buy beautiful things for herself. What she did have was a desire to make life better for herself and all Black people in the United States. Out of this impulse to improve, she created products that would help her start her own business, give her daughter an education, and create well-paying jobs for thousands of Black women across the country.

Sarah Breedlove was born on December 23, 1867, in Delta, Louisiana. She lived on a plantation, which is a large farm, with her parents, Minerva and Owen. She had five other siblings: older brothers Owen Jr., James, and Alex, younger brother Solomon, and a sister, Louvenia. Sarah's parents had been slaves before she was born, but they had achieved freedom during the Civil War, which ended in 1865.

Despite their newfound freedom, life was still very difficult for the Breedloves. When Sarah was growing up, the family worked on a cotton plantation as sharecroppers. They ran the plantation but they did not own it, and so had to give all the crops to their landlords. In reality, not much had changed for them since they had been slaves. They still worked for white men and had to struggle to make enough money to live. The children worked all day in the fields with their parents and then had to do chores in the evening.

At that time, it was almost impossible for a Black child to go to school in the southern United States. In some parts of Louisiana, schools were burned down and teachers were threatened if they tried to teach Black children. Many people who used to be slave owners were scared to have educated Black people around, because they thought the Black people might question the way things were done or begin to demand equal rights for themselves. Sarah, therefore, never had the chance to go to school.

If Sarah's life seemed difficult up until then, things were about to get even worse. In 1873, when Sarah was just six, her mother died, and about a year later, her father also passed away. No one knows for sure how they died, but it is thought to have been from yellow fever. Alex, the oldest child, moved to Vicksburg, Mississippi, to get a job. Louvenia married a man named Jesse Powell and Sarah moved in with the new couple. In 1877, the cotton crop failed and then there was another devastating outbreak of yellow fever. People could not afford to buy what little cotton Sarah, Louvenia, and Jesse had to sell. They decided to join Alex in Vicksburg, where they could find other jobs.

Living with Louvenia and Jesse was not easy for Sarah. Jesse had a bad temper and was angry that they had to look after young Sarah. He expected Sarah to work to help pay for food and bills. So Sarah worked as a laundress, washing clothes for other people. When she was just fourteen years old, Sarah married Moses McWilliams. She was able to move out of her sister's house and get away from Jesse, but the new couple did not have much money, so she kept working as a laundress. After three years, Sarah and Moses had a daughter, Lelia. Considering the hardships she had faced so far, things were beginning to look up for Sarah. Unfortunately, the good times would not last long. Moses died two years later. Sarah was at widow at twenty.

Sarah decided to leave Vicksburg in 1889 to live in St. Louis, Missouri. She had only enough money in her pocket for one-way tickets for herself and her daughter. Luckily, she knew some people in St. Louis who had offered to let Sarah and Lelia live with them. Alex, James, and Solomon had already settled in St. Louis and together owned a barbershop. St. Louis was very different from Vicksburg, where Black people could not even dream of owning their own businesses. Sarah continued to work as a laundress, a job that allowed her to look after Lelia at the same time. Sarah wanted Lelia to have all the opportunities that she had not been given, including the chance to go to school.

Sarah was determined to make a new start in St. Louis. She wanted to find a way to make more money for herself and her daughter. Cleaning clothes was physically difficult and didn't earn Sarah enough money to send Lelia to school. Sarah also worried about what would happen if she hurt her back and could no longer work.

Even though Sarah had the desire to improve her life, she didn't know where to start. The World's Fair, which came to St. Louis in 1905, gave her the inspiration she needed. At the fair, she heard many inspiring Black leaders speak. She was particularly impressed with Mrs. Margaret Murray Washington. Sarah thought Margaret was a smart woman who spoke eloquently and was well-groomed. Sarah wanted to be like her and decided she would start by improving the way she looked. Because she was always working so hard and did not have enough money to eat well, Sarah's hair had long ago begun to fall out. Now she wanted to do something about it. She tried many different creams and shampoos, but nothing worked. Then, one night she had a dream in which an African man told her what to use to make her hair grow back. When Sarah woke up, she set about finding all the ingredients—some of which came from Africa—and mixed up the tonic. Her hair grew back within a few weeks. Sarah could hardly believe it! She gave her tonic to friends and it helped them too. Now she was convinced that she had made something special.

Sarah wanted to start selling her hair treatment, but there was already a big company in St. Louis that sold a hair tonic called Wonder Hair Grower. Sarah decided to move to Denver, Colorado, to start up her business. She knew that she needed money to start making batches of her hair treatment, but she arrived in Denver with only $1.50 in savings. She quickly found a job as a cook for E. L. Scholtz, the owner of a big pharmacy. In her spare time, she began working on three products: Wonderful Hair Grower, Glossine, and Vegetable Shampoo. Sarah's products didn't just make hair grow—they also cleaned it and softened curls. All of her products were made specifically for Black women. These products allowed Black women with tight curls to wear the long, flowing hairstyles that were popular at the time. Right away, Sarah's products were popular. Her business grew even more when she took out ads in the *Colorado Statesman*, an African-American newspaper that is still published in Denver.

Sarah had a friend back in St. Louis, Charles Joseph Walker, who worked as a sales agent for a newspaper. They kept writing to each other after Sarah moved to Denver. Charles gave her advice on how to sell her products. Their friendship grew and Charles moved to Denver. They were married on January 4, 1906. Sarah officially changed her name to Mrs. C.J. Walker. She decided to put her new name on her products, adding "Madam" to make it sound more important and formal, a name people should trust.

C.J. decided, against her husband's advice, to go on a cross-country tour to sell her products. She was gone for eighteen months. During her trip, she visited towns all over the United States to hire and train other Black women to be sales agents for her company. It was the sales agents' job to let people

These hair products were just two of many hair-growing tonics, which were among the beauty aids developed and sold by Madam C.J. Walker.

know about C.J.'s hair treatment products. Then they could order them from her through the mail.

The strategy worked. By 1908, C.J.'s business had grown so much that she decided to move the headquarters to Pittsburgh, Pennsylvania, because the city was known for its industry and it was in a more central location within the country. This would make sending out her mail orders much easier. Her daughter Lelia helped set up a training school, called Lelia College, for the company's sales agents.

At the school, women were taught to become "hair culturists"—they learned about C.J.'s products and how to sell them door-to-door. The women wore uniforms of black skirts and white blouses. When people saw them on the street they all knew they were Madam C.J. Walker sales agents. C.J. was the first to set up this type of large-scale business. It was so successful that many other companies would copy the way she ran her business.

C.J.'s company continued to grow. She began selling cosmetics designed for Black women and hot combs that would straighten their hair (the opposite of a curling iron). She was getting so many orders that she needed to set up a permanent factory to make all her products. C.J. chose to move the company again, this time to Indianapolis, Indiana, because at that time, it was a large city known for its banking and industry. It was also the crossroads for eight railway systems, which would help spread her product across the country. She named her company the Walker College of Hair Culture and Walker Manufacturing Co. The move proved to be a smart decision. Just one year later, her company had 950 salespeople who each made $5 to $15 a day. In 1911, this was a lot of money. Most women working at the time were in

On Jan. 28, 1998, the United States Postal Service issued the Madam C.J. Walker Commemorative stamp as a part of its Black Heritage Series.

jobs that did not require a lot of education or training and which paid only about $45 per month. In addition to the factory, C.J. also set up a hair and manicure salon and another training school.

While her business was taking off, C.J.'s personal life was not going so well. She and Charles had many differing opinions about running the business. This caused a lot of problems in their marriage. After so many years of working hard for other people, C.J. wanted to make her own business decisions. C.J. and Charles were eventually divorced.

C.J. was no stranger to discrimination. All her life, she had been treated differently because she was Black—and even after she had become a successful businesswoman, it was no different. One day, while living in Indianapolis, she decided to go to the theater, but the ticket agent tried to charge her twice as much as everyone else. C.J. wouldn't stand for it. She immediately called a lawyer and sued the theater. Then, she began to draw up plans for her own entertainment building, called The Walker Building, a block-long building that housed a beauty salon, coffee shop, and a theater that opened a few years later.

C.J. wanted to expand her business even more and traveled to the Caribbean and Central America to sell her products. In 1916, she moved to Harlem, New York, to be closer to her daughter, who had moved there previously. C.J. kept the plant in Indianapolis and ran her business from a New York office. Things couldn't have been going better. Her company was selling over $250,000 in hair treatment products every year and employed more than 3,000 people in the production plant and more than 20,000 sales agents! C.J. had become one of America's first Black millionaires and America's first self-made female millionaire. She bought a thirty-four-room estate on the Hudson River in New York that was often used for conventions on civil rights. But Madam C.J. Walker wasn't done yet.

C.J. was an inspiration to other women in business. She gave lectures on Black issues at conventions sponsored by powerful Black institutions. She encouraged Black Americans to support the cause of World War I and worked to ensure that Black soldiers were not separated from white soldiers. She also argued that Black soldiers returning from the war as veterans should be granted full respect. In Harlem, C.J. began to get involved in the city's political life. She had been involved in other community projects before—in Indianapolis, she had donated $1,000 to help build a YMCA for the Black community—but now that her business was set, she began to devote more time and money to the causes she believed in. Relations between Black and white people in the United States were very hostile in places. There were many instances were Black people were being lynched (hanged) by white people—not illegal at the time! It was very difficult for C.J. to hear about these stories in the news.

This grand home, known as Villa Lewaro, was built by Madam C.J. Walker in Irvington, New York.

She joined the National Association for the Advancement of Colored People (NAACP), a civil rights organization, in its fight against these lynchings.

W.E.B Du Bois, a well-known civil rights activist and writer, wrote about C.J. after she had passed away, "It is given to few persons to transform a people in a generation. Yet this was done by the late Madam C.J. Walker."

In 1918, Woodrow Wilson was elected president of the United States. He was a segregationist, which means that he believed white and Black people should live completely separate from one another. He believed that they should go to different schools, shop in different stores, drink from different water fountains, and more. C.J. had grown up in a time when Black people had very few rights. She had managed to create her own successful business and take control of her life, but she still did not enjoy the same rights as a white person. C.J. had always donated her time and money to charitable organizations, but now she felt very strongly that she had to become active in politics to fight for the rights of Black people. In 1917, she had been one of many prominent Black activists to visit the White House in protest of segregation and lynching. C.J. and others brought a petition that asked the government to make lynching a federal crime.

C.J. inspired her employees to get involved in politics too. She created local and state clubs for her sales agents. In 1917, she had organized the Madam C.J. Walker Hair Culturists Union of America convention in Philadelphia. It may have been the first national meeting of businesswomen in the country. At the meeting, C.J. called on her agents not to sit by while unjust things, like the lynchings of Black men, continued to happen. She asked them to get involved, so that these things would not be allowed to continue.

C.J. passed away two years later, on May 25, 1919, in her home in New York. In her will she continued her support of Black issues by giving money to Black schools, organizations, individuals, orphanages, retirement homes, as well as Black YWCAs and YMCAs. Throughout her life, she had proved that you don't need to begin with much to achieve great things. While many of the important things in C.J.'s life had been taken from her or denied her, C.J. worked hard at everything she did and had faith that she could do something to make life better for herself, for Lelia, and for Black people in her country.

Chapter 2

Lise Meitner

1878–1968

Lise Meitner knew from a young age that she wanted to spend her life exploring science and making new discoveries. Despite some major obstacles that were thrown her way, she always managed to persevere and continue her work. She made many valuable discoveries, the most important of which was to observe and define a new process called nuclear fission. Though she didn't get much recognition for her work, that wasn't so important to her. She wanted to further science—not her own name.

Lise was born Elise Meitner in November of 1878 in Vienna, Austria. Her father, Phillip, was a lawyer who was active in politics. Phillip and his wife Hedwig were very open, intellectual, and generous. The Meitner home was an exciting place, with lots of lively conversation. Guests were always welcome and the house always seemed to be full of interesting people, such as writers, lawyers, and politicians. Lise, the third of eight children, was an inquisitive girl, and always curious about the world around her and how things worked. Fortunately, there were always plenty of people to ask in the Meitner house!

Lise enjoyed school very much, especially learning math. No matter where she was, she always seemed to have her math book somewhere close by. When Lise was growing up, it was normal for most girls to stop going to school at the age of fourteen. If a girl's parents could afford to continue her education, she could then attend a private teachers' college. Lise's parents sent her to a private school to learn how to be a French teacher, but this was not her passion. She knew she wanted to do something else. Luckily for Lise, attitudes were beginning to change. In the past, most universities had not admitted girls. Slowly, the schools were beginning to accept female students and Lise saw an opportunity to further her education. Because she did not possess the same education that a boy her age would have had, she needed to take extra classes in order to be ready for university. She took Greek, Latin, math, physics, botany, zoology, and many other courses. Lise was very fortunate that her parents were supportive and wealthy.

When she was twenty-three, Lise began studying at the University of Vienna. A serious student, she took classes in physics, calculus, chemistry, and botany, but soon found that physics was her favorite subject. She finished her courses in 1905, after three years of study, and immediately started her doctorate. Lise received her PhD in physics in 1906.

After graduation, it was difficult for Lise to find a job. There were not many opportunities for physicists to begin with, let alone for a female physicist. Lise had to take a teaching job at a girls' school. She did not really like teaching, and longed to be back at work in the science lab. After work, she often went to the university to help her friend Stefan Meyer, the director of the Physics Institute, with his experiments.

In 1907, Lise went to study with Max Planck, a brilliant physicist, and do research at the Friederic-Wilhelm-Universitat, a university in Berlin, Germany. Attitudes toward women were not as open in Germany as they were in Austria, and Lise had to ask permission to do research at the university. She was accepted and moved to Berlin. There, Lise met Otto Hahn, a chemist who would become her future lab partner. Lise and Otto were both very interested in radioactivity; their background and experiences complemented one another. They worked well together.

Lise worked side by side with Otto Hahn on their experiments, but because she was a woman, she wasn't paid for her work. Her parents continued to send her money so that she could stay in Berlin. In 1913, Lise was finally offered a paying job. She and Otto worked at the new radioactivity section of the Kaiser-Wilhelm-Institute, a university outside of Berlin. Lise and Otto were a good team and together they made many discoveries. To honor them, the new building was named the Laboratorium Hahn-Meitner. Lise was now making money, but she was paid less than Otto, even though they held the same job.

The next year, when World War I began, Otto left the lab to fight in the war. Lise, wanting to help out in some way, signed up for X-ray technician training and other courses so

In 1982, a new element called Meitnerium was named in Lise's honor.

she could work in the medical corps. She helped doctors during operations, cleaned tables and medical instruments, and bandaged wounded patients. While she wanted to help the doctors, she could not stop thinking about her experiments and how much she wanted to get back to her research. In 1916, she returned to the lab and continued her work. Otto helped out when he could during his short breaks from service in the army, but mostly Lise worked alone. It was very hard to continue her research during this time since many of the materials she needed for her experiments were being used for the war. Even things like food and fuel were hard to find.

In 1917, Lise received a promotion—the Hahn-Meitner lab was split in two and she got her own lab. Lise and Otto continued to keep in touch, even when he was away at war. They sent each other long letters, discussing her experiments. In a letter dated January 17, 1918, Lise wrote to tell Otto that she had discovered a new element, protactinium, which they had been trying to find for a long time. The two scientists wrote an article announcing the discovery and protactinium (Pa) was added to the periodic table. Lise had done almost all the work on her own, but Otto Hahn was named as "senior author" on all their articles. It would not be the last time Otto received the credit for some of Lise's ideas and hard work.

In 1919, Lise was promoted to Physics Professor and became the first woman in Germany to be named a professor. Life after the war was very difficult. Everything—even basic necessities like butter, eggs, and milk—was either very expensive or hard to find. Lise was grateful to have a job and for the care packages of coffee and cake her mother would send from Austria.

Though life was hard for most people, it was an exciting time in physics. Scientists were making new discoveries every day. Lise was inspired by the work of her colleagues and continued to create new experiments. For one of these experiments, she made a cloud chamber—a sealed container filled with air that was moist and dense like a cloud. Little drops of water formed on any particles, such as atoms, in the chamber. Lise set up a camera to take pictures of the tracks made by the particles as they moved through the air. This helped her study the behavior of the atoms and nuclei.

In 1933, the Nazi Party came into power in Germany and ordered Kaiser-Wilhelm-Institute to fire all Jewish scientists. The director of the institute, Fritz Haber, resigned in protest. Otto Hahn took on Fritz's job and was faced with the same pressure. Many scientists left to work in England or the United States. In September 1933 Lise, being of Jewish descent, was not allowed to teach anymore, but she was permitted to keep up her research. Even though Lise had converted to Protestantism as a child, she was still seen as Jewish by the German government. She received a lot of pressure to resign, even from her good friend Otto.

She wrote to her fellow scientists in other countries in Europe to see if she could find a job. It was very difficult for Lise to find a country that would let her visit, even for a short time, and the German government did not want to let Jewish people out of the country. Finally, she was offered a position in Sweden. Her friends and fellow physicists Dirk Foster and Adriaan Fokker helped get her out of Germany. Lise had to leave quickly, taking only a few clothes and some money. Otto gave her a diamond ring he had inherited from his mother so that she could sell it if she ran out of money.

Though Lise was grateful to be out of Germany, she was disappointed in her new job as a researcher at the Nobel Institute for Experimental Physics in Sweden. Instead of her normal salary, Lise was given barely enough money to live on. The lab was poorly equipped and her new colleague, Manne Siegbahn, the director of the institute, was much younger than she was. He thought her ideas were outdated and didn't regard her as an equal in their field. He didn't include her in his work or give her the equipment and the assistants she needed to set up her own lab. Since she had left home so quickly, she hadn't brought much with her, and didn't even have her books or clothes for the winter.

In the meantime, back in Germany, Otto Hahn was continuing on with the experiments that he and Lise had started together, along with Fritz Strassman. One day, Otto and Fritz met secretly with Lise in Copenhagen to discuss their findings. They had been experimenting on an element called uranium and had created a new substance from it. Otto Hahn and Fritz thought the new radioactive mixture was an isotope (a different form) of radium.

But Lise was not so sure. She believed that the new substance was barium, another element, and that Otto Hahn and Fritz had broken the uranium into barium. Spurred on by her ideas, Otto Hahn and Fritz kept on with their experiments. Otto Hahn eventually wrote a letter to Lise asking her to help figure out if a uranium atom could be split.

Lise shared the letter with her nephew, Otto Robert Frisch, who was also a physicist. He had

"It was an unfortunate accident that this discovery came about in time of war. I myself have not worked on smashing the atom with the idea of producing death-dealing weapons. Women have a great responsibility and they are obliged to try so far as they can to prevent another war"
— Lise Meitner
Mothers of Invention

come to see his aunt because he wanted to discuss an experiment of his own. Instead, he became caught up in Lise's own scientific puzzle. Using their combined knowledge of physics and math, Lise and Otto Robert were able to prove that an atom could indeed be split in two. Back in Germany, Otto Hahn and Fritz Strassman published an article announcing that they had split an atom. They did not put Lise's name on the article; the Nazi government had banned them from working with her because she was Jewish. Lise and her nephew, Otto Robert, published another article explaining how it could be done. Lise called the process nuclear fission.

This was big news in the physics world, but Lise received little recognition for her discovery. The director at the institute never congratulated her or offered her equipment or support

Lise Meitner and Otto Hahn meet again at the 1959 opening of the Hahn-Meitner Institute for Nuclear Research in Berlin, Germany.

for the many other follow-up experiments she wanted to do. Even more difficult for Lise was the fact that Otto Hahn had claimed full credit for splitting the atom. He said that he and Lise had never discussed physics—that it was his work as a chemist alone that led him to split the atom. This hurt Lise very much. They had been close friends for a long time and without Lise's ideas, Otto and Fritz never would have been able to split the atom, because even though Lise lived far away in Sweden, she was the intellectual leader of their team.

Lise's work life in Sweden continued to be very difficult, so when she had an opportunity to work in Denmark, she took it. World War II was underway by this time and when Germany invaded Denmark the country quickly surrendered. Lise had to return to Sweden, where she focused on helping Jews escape from Germany and Austria. Lise was outspoken against Hitler and the war and was frustrated by some of her friends, such as Otto, who were not so bold.

People soon began to understand the power of Lise's nuclear fission. When atoms were split, they created a lot of power. Scientists realized that if they could somehow harness the power of millions of splitting atoms, they could make a very dangerous bomb. The United States, England, and Germany were all trying to be the first to make such a bomb. Even Lise's nephew, Otto Robert, was working on a project to build a bomb in England. He had been invited to go to the United States and made sure that Lise was asked also, but she refused.

In 1944, Otto Hahn was awarded the Nobel Prize for discovering nuclear fission. No one from Germany was allowed to accept awards during the war, so it was kept a secret. Lise was totally ignored.

On August 7, 1945, Lise received a call from a reporter who told her that a nuclear bomb had been dropped by the United States army in Hiroshima, Japan. Lise was devastated to hear what her discovery of nuclear fission had been used to do. The bomb had killed between 70,000 and 100,000 people and destroyed three square miles (eight square kilometers) of land. At that point, Lise received a lot of attention, more than she had ever wanted and for something she had never intended to be a part of.

In 1955, Lise won the Otto Hahn prize, named after her old friend. In 1958, an institute for nuclear research was built outside Berlin in Germany. At first, they wanted to name it after Otto Hahn, but Lise had many supporters and they spoke up on her behalf. In the end, the building was named after both scientists and became the Hahn-Meitner Institute for Nuclear Research.

Lise finally left the institute in Sweden for a new job in 1947 at the Royal Institute of Technology in Sweden. This time she had her own lab and her director, Gudmund Borelius, was happy to have her there and supported her work wholeheartedly. Lise liked her new job but never felt fully at home in Sweden. At the same time, she realized she could never return to Germany. She felt that some people in Germany still did not take full responsibility for what had happened during the war and that was something she could not live with.

Lise continued her research until she was in her seventies. Most of her work focused on using nuclear fission to produce energy. She helped build Sweden's first nuclear reactor (a way of using nuclear fission to create energy for electricity, for example) and helped recruit young students and researchers.

She retired from research in 1954, when she was seventy-five. She kept up with her reading on new research in her field, though, and spent a lot of time writing. When she was eighty-two, Lise moved to England to be closer to her nephew, Otto Robert, and his family. When Lise, Otto Hahn, and Fritz Strassman were awarded the U.S. Atomic Energy

Commission's Enrico Fermi Award for their contributions to nuclear fission in 1966, Lise was too ill to accept her prize. Instead, her nephew traveled to Vienna to accept the honor on her behalf. Even at this point, Otto Hahn denied that Lise had contributed to the discovery. It is a version of events that he held on to until his death in 1968.

Lise's health continued to falter and she died on October 27, 1968, at the age of eighty-nine, not long after Otto Hahn passed away. Even though she did not get the credit she deserved, Lise's lifelong dedication to science led to major discoveries that have shaped the way we live today.

Chapter 3

Lillian Moller Gilbreth

1878–1972

Lillian Moller grew up in a busy household where she had many responsibilities. Maybe it was growing up with seven younger brothers and sisters that made her want to have a large family of her own. Whatever the reason, it was a good thing Lillian was an organized person and liked to take care of others. She was very good at finding the most efficient way to do things, and used this skill to make several useful inventions that would help women make the most of their time. In Lillian's time, most women worked at home, taking care of the family and running the household. Though they weren't paid for their work, it was a very demanding job. With twelve children of her own, Lillian knew this quite well! She dedicated her time to helping other women get more out of theirs.

Lillie Evelyn Moller was born in Oakland, California, on May 24, 1878. She was the first child for her parents, William Moller and Annie Delger Moller. Lillie was very close to both her parents, but especially to her father. He would often take her into town with him when he had errands to run. Lillie wasn't the only child in the house for long. When she was two years old, her mother had a second child, Gertie. Then one of her aunts came to live with the Mollers, along with her five children. Over the next several years Lillie's mother had six more children, making the family even bigger. With so many children in the home, Lillie had to help look after some of the younger ones.

Lillie was educated at home by her parents until she was nine. When the time came for her to go to school, she was not happy. A shy child, she felt more comfortable being at home with her family. She had to start school in Grade One, but since she was used to taking care of younger children, she didn't mind so much being around the younger students—in fact, she often helped the teacher look after them. Lillie did well in school, but even though her grades were good, she didn't have many friends. Then, when she went to high school, things began to get better for Lillie. She changed her name to Lillian to sound more grown up, and began to believe in herself. By her last year of high school, Lillian was the vice-president of her class and graduated with straight A's.

Lillian went on to the University of California at Berkley, earning a bachelor's degree in English literature in 1900. At her graduation, she was the first woman to speak at the commencement of any branch of the University of California. She went on to earn her master's degree in literature. When she graduated in 1902, she wasn't sure what to do next, so she was very happy when schoolteacher Minnie Bunker invited her to go on a tour of Europe.

In June 1903, she took a train across the country with her friend Eva to meet Minnie in Boston. There, she was introduced to Minnie's cousin Frank Gilbreth, a building contractor. Over the next few days in the city, Lillian visited Minnie's family and friends and had many interesting conversations with Frank. They were both intellectual people and enjoyed joking with each other. Soon the women had to set off on their trip to Europe, so Lillian said good-bye to her new friend. When she returned to the U.S. in November, Frank, along with her parents, met the boat in New York. Frank was very interested in Lillian, but first he had to convince her parents that he could support their daughter. Lillian traveled with her parents back out West by train. Frank joined them soon after and proposed to Lillian with the blessing of her parents. Then he returned to the East Coast and Lillian didn't see him again until ten months later, when he came for their wedding.

Frank and Lillian were very different people. Frank was outgoing and lighthearted. When he graduated from high school he had decided to take a job right away. He did not want to go to university. At first, it was difficult for him to deal with the fact that Lillian was more highly educated. But soon he began to value her skills. During their time apart before the wedding, they wrote to each other every day and Lillian gave him advice on advertising and other parts of his business.

Once they were married, Lillian had to move to New York to live with Frank and his mother, Martha, and

Lillian knew that she wanted to go to college, but when she first asked her father, he said no. It wasn't because he thought she couldn't do it, though. William knew his daughter was smart and capable. But the family had a lot of money and he thought women only went to school if they needed to make money (usually as a teacher). Since the Moller girls didn't need to work to have money, their father thought they shouldn't go to college. Lillian wouldn't give up, though, and eventually her father allowed her to go.

Two of Lillian's children, Ernestine and Frank Jr., wrote a book about their home life with twelve children, called *Cheaper by the Dozen*. The book was published in 1948 and two years later, it was made into a movie. Lillian wasn't given full credit in the movie for being the smart, hard-working inventor that she was. Instead, the film focused on her being a mother, while Frank was seen as the efficiency expert.

his Aunt Kit. This was very difficult for Lillian and she struggled to find her place in her new home. Martha and Kit were clearly in charge of the household, which at that time would normally be a wife's role. Frank wanted Lillian to work with him but not in the office. So she worked in the study of their home, reading about different construction skills and techniques, like mixing concrete and laying brick. She began to write books about these different techniques and innovations. Lillian was very good at thinking of better, easier, and faster ways to do things, and though she had no previous experience in construction, she had no trouble understanding the material and applying her skills to a new subject.

Lillian loved to work, but in 1905 she had her first baby, Anne, and had to change her life to take on this new responsibility. With Frank often away from home on business, Lillian had to manage the raising of their children. Lillian loved children and being a mother. In fact, she had one baby almost every fifteen months from 1905 until 1922 for a total of twelve!

1907 was an eventful year for Lillian and Frank. They met Frederick Winslow Taylor, a man known as the father of scientific management. He was famous for thinking of new ways that people in factories could save time and money. Lillian didn't agree with all of his ideas, but she learned a lot from him. He may have been what inspired her to go back to school for her PhD in educational psychology.

Lillian and Frank worked on the same topic as Taylor. They tried to think of ways that people could work that would save time and money. They did motion studies to figure out the best way to do a task. Frank took still photos of Lillian performing certain tasks that factory workers performed, and then they would analyze the photos to see how the tasks could be done more efficiently. They would pay attention to how far Lillian had to reach to pick up an object or how many individual movements she would have to make in order to complete a task. Then they would change where things were placed or how they were built so that the number and range of movements needed was lessened. Lillian believed that changing your movements could make a big difference in how much time and effort you needed to get work done.

In 1910, Frank and Lillian went on a trip to England to attend the joint meeting of the American Society of Mechanical Engineers and the British Institution of Mechanical Engineers. Lillian was happy because Taylor mentioned her work on the psychology of management in his speech at the conference. It surprised most people there because they all thought of Lillian as just Frank's wife. Now they were beginning to realize that she had her own ideas.

In 1910, Lillian had her fifth child and first son, Frank Jr. The family was very happy, especially Frank Sr. Unfortunately, in 1912, they lost their five-year-old daughter Mary to diphtheria, an infectious disease that starts in the mouth and throat, but can move to the nerves and heart, causing death. Frank and Lillian were devastated.

Despite their loss, they tried to move on. Lillian wanted to finish her degree but was told that she had to spend a year at the University of California in order to graduate. She did not want to move her family and refused. Instead, she published the paper she had been working on, "The Psychology of Management," and looked for another school. Lillian found

Brown University in Providence, Rhode Island, and studied applied management. She received her PhD in Psychology in 1915. Lillian and Frank wrote several books together about efficiency and management, including *Concrete System* (1908), *Bricklaying System* (1909), *Motion Study* (1911), and *A Primer of Scientific Management* (1912). Lillian was not named as an author because the publishers didn't want people to know that a woman had been involved in the ideas.

Not long afterward, Frank decided to give up his business so the two of them could start their own company together. They became management consultants, which means companies paid them to look at the way their workers performed their tasks. Then Frank and Lillian would tell them how it could be done better in order to save money and time. What made Lillian's

The Gilbreth family assembles for a family portrait, with Lillian and Frank seated in the center. Their large family and efficient management of home life was the inspiration for the book Cheaper by the Dozen, *which has been adapted for film several times.*

ideas unique was that she included the psychological happiness of the workers in the design of the tasks. She understood that if a worker was overtired, stressed, or unhappy, then his or her working ability was reduced. This is now referred to as industrial-organizational psychology and Lillian was the first person to identify it.

Though Lillian designed efficient kitchens to help women make better use of their time, she didn't spend much time in her own kitchen. Lillian had grown up with servants and was not a good cook. She also had a very inefficient and old-fashioned kitchen. As her children said, "Lillie and kitchens were natural enemies. She hated them and they retaliated. Stoves burned her, ice picks stabbed her, graters skinned her, and paring knives cut her."

When World War I began, Lillian had to run the business on her own for a while. Frank decided he wanted to help out in the war, so he went to the School of Artillery at Fort Still, Oklahoma. He made training films on efficient ways to load a rifle or care for a horse. He sent films and papers home to Lillian for her to analyze.

On March 1, 1918, Lillian received a telegram that Frank was sick. She left as soon as she could, but it took her two days by train to get to Oklahoma. She cared for him in the hospital for seven weeks. Frank recovered somewhat, but he was weak and couldn't do as much work afterward. This meant that Lillian had to take on more.

Frank never fully recovered and in 1924, he died. Lillian now had to support their eleven children all by herself. She began to work harder than ever, sometimes for ten hours a day, six or seven days a week. To make more money for her family, Lillian decided to start teaching courses in motion study and scientific management.

Lillian continued to write, and published a book called *Quest of the One Best Way*, which was an account of her family experiment. With so many children, Lillian had to manage her time and household tasks very carefully. She had everything planned out and the children each had their own jobs to do at specific times during the day.

Lillian started to become a bit of a celebrity, well known as the woman who could do it all—raise a big family and run her own business. She gave speeches at many different universities and women's groups. She would say that women should do what they were best at. This could be either paid work outside the home, or inside, as a wife, mother, and housekeeper. Lillian thought women should try to do both. Too often women were told that they have to give up marriage and a family if they wanted a career, but Lillian proved that this was untrue.

People considered Lillian an expert in women's work. In 1926, she wrote *The Home-maker and Her Job*. The book was designed to help women find efficient ways of doing their housework so that they would have time for other things. Lillian felt that one of the things that made housework work was that kitchens were designed by men, who never had to use them. She thought that if a woman, who uses a kitchen all the time and knows what works and what doesn't, could design a kitchen, it would make the job of cooking and cleaning much easier.

Lillian continued to work as a speaker and a consultant for different companies. Mary Dillion, the head of the Brooklyn Borough Gas Company, asked her to design an efficient kitchen, called Kitchen Practical. Lillian created a circular workspace, with everything placed where it would be easiest and fastest for women to perform their most common duties. She was then asked to design three more kitchens. She positioned the stove, the refrigerator, and the sink so that the actions needed to move between them were reduced. She also changed the level of the counter to reduce back strain. For these kitchens, she designed many time-saving gadgets, like the garbage can with a foot lever to lift up the lid, and a planning desk. The desk is perhaps her favorite and best-known invention. It had a shelf for recipes and nutrition books, a place to put bills that need to be paid and those that need to be filed away, and a tool drawer with a hammer, nails, screws, and other handy things for minor repairs. The desk even came with a telephone because Lillian thought it was so important.

Lillian Moller Gilbreth was known as the "mother of modern management."

In 1926, Lillian became the first woman to become a member of the American Society of Mechanical Engineers. She continued to work as a consultant, but the 1930s were a difficult time to find work and make money. It was especially hard to do contract work, so she lived in the women's residence hall and would have breakfast every morning with any students who got up early enough to join her. In 1937, she cut down on her work and moved out of the residence, but she remained a part-time professor at Purdue for many years.

Lillian continued to work, first as an advisor to the government during World War II, then after the war, as an efficiency expert in hospitals, helping to find the best way to organize hospital supplies and determining the best equipment to use. When she was in her late seventies, Lillian began to work on a very important project called "handicapped homemakers." She designed the Heart Kitchen, for women with health or mobility problems. She wanted to show them how to set up the kitchen so that things were within easy reach and how they could save time and precious energy in their tasks.

Lillian Gilbreth inspects office machinery during a 1958 lecture stop at Washington University in St. Louis, MO.

In 1953, she went on a six-month trip that took her to Australia, the Philippines, Hong Kong, India, England, and Brazil. She visited hospitals, schools, and people to discuss her work and she analyzed how people lived. It would be the first of many world tours she would take during the next ten years. Lillian worked until 1968, when she was forced to stop under doctor's orders. In 1969, she fell and broke her hip. She never fully recovered and on January 2, 1972, she died.

Lillian's inventions gave people one of the most valuable things in their busy lives—time. A tireless worker, she spent most of her time trying to find ways for other people to find more time in their own lives. Her work was especially important for other women, many of whom spent a lot of time working in the home, taking care of their families. With her time-saving devices and ideas for making work spaces more efficient, Lillian gave these women (and other people, too) a little bit of freedom to pursue the things they wanted to do, but could never seem to find the time for.

Lillian Gilbreth presents the Lillian Moller Gilbreth Scholarship to Valerie Petersen, a nuclear engineer student, in 1964.

Chapter 4

Elizabeth Muriel MacGill

1905–1980

It seems that everyone is born with both certain advantages and disadvantages in life. We all have things that help us (maybe a special talent or a family member, friend, or teacher who inspires us to chase our dreams) and other things that seem to hold us back, obstacles we have to work hard to overcome. It is especially difficult, though, when the challenges we face have been created by other people's ideas of what we can and cannot do. Sometimes you may have an idea of something you would like to do or make, but other people don't believe it can be done or that you are capable of doing it. This can be very discouraging, and you may even want to give up.

Elsie was born in a loving household, to a wealthy family that could afford to give her the education she needed to fulfill her dreams. The obstacles she faced were created by the attitudes of other people toward her. They would later wonder how she could design planes, manage a large company, or how she could start her own business. Elsie did all of this and much, much more. Her secret was to believe in herself and never give up. Elsie also believed that all women had everything they needed, inside of them, to do all the things they wanted to do—they just had to realize it.

Elsie was born Elizabeth Muriel MacGill in Vancouver, British Columbia, on March 27, 1905. Her father, James Henry MacGill, was a lawyer, and her mother, Helen, was a judge. Helen was the first woman in British Columbia to become a judge and she was a big influence on Elsie. As a judge, she worked very hard to change legislation in Canada in order to improve the lives of women and children. Before becoming a judge, Helen had been a journalist. She had traveled throughout western Canada and even to Japan on her own. She had to be a very strong woman to do that type of work, and without a doubt she was Elsie's role model.

Elsie had a very good childhood. Her parents were both successful in their careers, and money was not a problem for the family. Elsie even took art lessons from the famous Canadian artist Emily Carr. Emily wasn't very famous then, and Elsie was far from an accomplished artist. Helen enrolled Elsie in art lessons, not so much because Elsie showed artistic talent, but because Helen wanted to support Emily Carr financially so that she could keep on painting. Elsie's parents were very progressive in their thinking; they believed in ideas that were new and not always popular at the time. Elsie learned that it was okay to be different from other people and to have ideas that others, perhaps, didn't agree with.

Throughout her life, Elsie continued her mother's tradition of breaking new ground. After high school, she moved to Toronto to study engineering at the University of Toronto. In 1927, she became the first woman in Canada to earn a degree as

Elsie MacGill graduated from the University of Toronto in 1927, becoming the first woman in Canada to earn a degree as an electrical engineer.

an electrical engineer. Elsie then got a job at the Austin Automobile Company in Pontiac, Michigan. The company started out making cars, but later began producing aircrafts. This sparked in Elsie an interest in aeronautics, the study, design, and manufacturing of planes and other machines that fly. Elsie was so interested in the subject that she decided to go back to school. She attended the University of Michigan, and, in 1929, she became the first woman to gain a master's degree in aeronautical engineering.

Elsie's success in school is even more impressive given her health problems at the time. In 1929, she came down with polio, which is a disease that causes a person's muscles to become very weak and can even lead to paralysis. Today, there is a vaccine for polio, but at the time, it was a very serious illness. Elsie got polio just a few weeks before her final year of school at the University of Michigan. She became unable to walk by herself, and so was forced to go home to recover before she was finished with school. Even though she didn't take her final exams, she still earned her degree because of the hard work she had done over the previous four years.

Things did not look good for Elsie. The doctors told her she would never be able to walk again. That wasn't going to stop Elsie from doing what she wanted. While she was recovering, she spent her time writing articles on aviation. For a while, she had to use a wheelchair because her muscles were not strong enough for her to walk, but she was still determined to walk some day. She worked very hard and eventually could walk with the help of two canes.

At this point Elsie decided to go back to school and enrolled at the Massachusetts Institute of Technology in Boston. After earning her master's degree in aeronautical engineering, she got a job at Fairchild Aircraft Ltd. in Montreal. There, she helped design the first all-metal aircraft ever built in Canada. It was at Fairchild that Elsie began to make a name for herself in the world of aircraft design. She represented the company at the National Research Council of Canada, where they test the planes before they can be used.

In 1938, Elsie became the first woman corporate member of the Engineering Institute of Canada. That same year, she moved to Canadian Car and Foundry Co. Ltd. (also called Can-Car) and became Chief Aeronautical Engineer. She was excited to have such an important job so early in her career and was very committed to making valuable contributions to her field.

At Can-Car, Elsie designed the Maple Leaf Trainer II, a plane used to teach pilots how to fly. It was the first female-designed aircraft in the world. The Maple Leaf Trainer II was a two-seat fabric-covered plane. It earned a Certificate of Airworthiness, Acrobatic Category (which means it was safe to fly), in only eight months, which was a record. At that time, no other plane had been given the certificate so quickly. Elsie also oversaw the testing of the plane. She had always wanted to be a pilot but couldn't fly a plane because of the damage done to her legs by polio. Still, she always insisted on being a passenger on all test flights, because she believed that was the best way to figure out whether anything needed to be improved.

Elsie's responsibilities grew greatly when World War II broke out and Can-Car began making planes for the British government to use in the war. Elsie was in charge of making the Hawker Hurricane fighter planes. The plant originally had only a few hundred workers but when production began for the war, Elsie was managing about 4,500 workers. There weren't enough trained workers available to make as many planes as quickly as they needed them for the war, so Elsie had to hire many people who had no experience working on planes, or even in a factory. Since many men had gone off to fight overseas,

At the height of Elsie's fame working at Can-Car during the war, a comic book was made about her called *Queen of the Hurricanes*. It told the story of how Elsie became an engineer, describing all the challenges she faced as a woman and as someone with a physical disability. Many of the scenes in the book were not true, such as one in which Elsie is shown stopping work in the factory to rescue a kitten from one of the machines.

she began to hire women to work in the factory. Before that time, people had said that women couldn't work with machines or in a factory, but when the war started, it became accepted. In Fort William, where the plant was located, many girls were only able to go to school up until Grade 8. There weren't many choices for those who couldn't afford to continue their studies. One option was to get a job as a maid, which paid just $10 per month. In contrast, a job as a welder at Elsie's factory paid $80 per month—and Elsie's job paid $350 per month! For many women, working at Can-Car during the war was the first chance they'd ever had to make a good wage.

Elsie designed more than just the Maple Leaf Trainer II. When the company began making planes for the war, they had to update the factory. Elsie supervised the changes, and oversaw the design and manufacturing of the special tools and equipment they needed to make the plane parts. The British government had very strict rules about how the planes should be made, and it was part of Elsie's job to make sure these standards were met. Elsie even designed a special variation of the Hawker Hurricane plane that had skis and de-icers, so that it would be safe to fly in colder climates.

It was hard to find materials during the war to make the planes, but still they managed. By the end of the war, they had made about 1,400 Hawker Hurricanes. Elsie's position in the company attracted a lot of attention, and many newspaper articles were written about her. They didn't always focus on her work, though. Instead, they talked about her looks and the fact that she was a woman. Headlines said things like, "She Debates Plane Design Just Like Recipe for Pie" and "New War Plane Designer Is Slim Girl with Curls." The articles noted that Elsie liked to cook, play cards, knit, and have afternoon tea. Many people couldn't understand how a woman could be such an accomplished engineer and manage so many employees, so they needed to hear things about Elsie that were more traditionally "feminine," like how pretty she was or what she liked to cook. Elsie knew that her work was important and she was good at it, no matter what other people said or thought. Elsie did receive some recognition from her work. In 1941, she received

Elsie MacGill and her future husband, Bill Soulsby, stand beside one of Elsie's Maple Leaf Trainers at an airfield in Thunder Bay, Ontario, in 1939.

the Gzowski Medal of the Engineering Institute of Canada. It probably meant more to her to have her engineering ideas honored than to be famous in the media.

In 1942, the British government decided to stop using the Hawker Hurricane, and Elsie's factory had to find another plane to make. When the United States joined the war, they needed help making planes, so Can-Car took on the job of making a new bomber plane called the Helldiver. The plane was so new that they hadn't even finished designing it before the plant went into production. They would send design updates to the factory as they thought of them (50,000 updates in total!). The workers would have to change the way the planes were made right in the middle of making them. All the workers, including Elsie, worked overtime to get the 800 Helldiver planes ready.

When the war ended, many of the women who had worked in factories like Can-Car had to give up their jobs. Of the thousands of women at Can-Car, only three were kept on. But Elsie's influence was felt by every woman who worked for her. When her employees saw how hard Elsie worked, they realized that if she could be successful, they could too. Many were inspired by Elsie to find other work once they left the factory.

In 1943, Elsie was let go from her job at Can-Car. The company told its workers that she was not on schedule with the Helldiver, but there was another side to the story. Elsie had become friends with Bill Soulsby, the line-production manager at Can-Car. They had become very close and her bosses did not think this was appropriate. Bill was also fired from Can-Car, but it really didn't bother either of them. They were married a week after they left Can-Car and, true to her independent spirit, Elsie kept her own last name and stayed a MacGill. The couple moved to Toronto, where Elsie started her own aeronautical engineering company.

She worked as a consultant, giving design advice to other companies and governments. In 1946, she became the first woman to be a technical advisor to the United Nations' International Civil Aviation Organization. Since the United Nations (UN) has representatives from countries all over the world, Elsie's work had a wide-ranging influence. She helped create rules and guidelines for the design and production of commercial planes. The following year, she became the chairperson of the Stress Analysis Committee for the UN, making her the first woman to chair a committee in the UN. She had a lot of experience testing and designing airplanes and was highly qualified for the position.

Elsie had always believed that women were equal to men and could do any of the things that men can do. She realized, however, that not all women had the advantages that she had while growing up. Not all women came from wealthy families that could provide their education. Elsie also benefited from her mother's strength and support, but not all women had the same encouragement from their parents to pursue all the things they wanted from life. As a result, in the 1960s, Elsie began to help other women obtain the same opportunities as men were given. She volunteered for many different women's groups. From 1962 to 1964, she was the national president of the Canadian Federation of Business and Professional Women's Clubs. In 1967, she became the only feminist commissioner on the Royal Commission on the Status of Women in Canada.

Once again, Elsie had views that differed from those of the people around her. There were seven other members of the Royal Commission, but often Elsie did not agree with any of them. Disagreements occurred so often that Elsie wrote her own report. It described all the things she believed should be done to help women become equal to men in Canadian society. In 1970, Elsie left the commission but continued to work on behalf of women as a member of the Ontario Status of Women Committee and through her work in other national women's groups. She also set up the National Action Committee, a group whose goal is to make sure the Royal Commission on the Status of Women does a good job. In 1971, in recognition of her achievements in aeronautics and her dedication to improving the lives of women and children, Elsie received the Order of Canada, an award given to people who have worked hard to make Canada a better country.

Elsie died on November 4, 1980, in a car accident in Cambridge, Massachusetts. She had lived a life full of opportunity and support, but also lived through very difficult times. Elsie knew how lucky she was to have the love and encouragement of her family and she wished that all women could have that same support. She also knew how difficult it is when people do not believe in you. Not everyone she met believed that a woman could be an engineer and designer of planes. Others thought that a woman who needed canes to get around would not be able to keep up. Elsie did more than just keep up. She proved that it is possible for a woman to do anything she wants, if she has determination and drive. She also showed that having a physical disability does not mean that a person—man or woman—cannot achieve great things. Not only did Elsie achieve great things in her own life, but she gave much of her time and effort to helping other women fulfill their own dreams.

Chapter 5

Hedy Lamarr

1914–2000

Hedy Lamarr was born Hedwig Eva Maria Kiesler on November 9, 1914, in Vienna, Austria. Her father, Emil, was the director of a bank and her mother, Gertrude, was a concert pianist. When Hedy was born, Gertrude stopped working and devoted herself to being an at-home mother. Hedy grew up in a very loving household. An only child, she was given a lot of attention and earned the nickname "little Princess Hedy" within her family. She was especially close to her father, who spent hours telling her fairy tales or taking long walks with her.

When she was young, Hedy's parents made sure that she learned a variety of things. She went to ballet lessons, piano lessons, and had many tutors who helped her with her schoolwork. She also had a nanny who taught Hedy several languages. But while she enjoyed learning different languages, Hedy didn't really enjoy most of her other lessons. She went to a private school and then a girls' academy in Switzerland, but ran away many times.

Hedy showed an interest in acting from a very young age. She spent most of her money on magazines about movies and movie stars. She would read them and dream of one day becoming an actress. Hedy wasn't the type of girl to just dream, though; she was determined to make her dream a reality. Every day on the way to school, she walked by Sascah Film Studios. Eventually, she devised a plan. She wrote herself a permission slip to leave school and snuck into the studio. Once inside, she overheard a director named Alexis Granowsky telling someone that he needed to find an actor to play a small part in one of his movies. Hedy, charming and full of confidence, convinced Alexis to let her try out for the part. She had no acting experience at all, so it was no surprise that she did not do well. Still, Alexis saw some talent in the teenager and thought that one day she could be a good actress. He cast her in his movie.

Now all Hedy had to do was to convince her parents to let her take the part. It would mean dropping out of school, something that her parents would definitely disapprove of. But her father could never say no to her. Hedy was his little princess, after all. Emil thought that Hedy would soon give up on acting and go back to school. Things took a different turn, though.

Hedy took roles in more movies and even in some plays, where her acting was better. She moved to Berlin, Germany, to continue to improve her skills at a famous acting school run by Max Reinhardt, an actor and director. In 1933, at the age of eighteen, Hedy gained some fame when she starred in her fourth movie, *Ecstasy*. In this movie, Hedy had to appear in a scene without any clothes on. When she had accepted the role, the nude scene was not in the script. The director had added it in later, then threatened Hedy when she refused to do it. In the end, she gave in. When she went to see the movie with her parents, they were shocked and walked out of the movie. Hedy did not ever want to be in another film, but because of this movie, her life changed forever. *Ecstasy* was banned in the United States for many years, but people now knew her name.

On August 10, 1933, Hedy married her first husband, Fritz Mandl, whom she had met backstage at one of her plays. Fritz was the head of a company that made guns, shells, and grenades. He knew many famous people who came to visit and discuss the company's business. Hedy listened and observed Fritz's plans to design remote-controlled torpedoes and other military gear. He never made these torpedoes, however, because it was too easy for the remote-control system to be interrupted. The enemy could figure out the path of the torpedo and change its course. This is a problem that Hedy would remember and think about for years. Even though the marriage was an unhappy one, the experience would turn out to be valuable to Hedy later in life—it proved to be the inspiration for her invention.

Hedy's unhappiness with her marriage stemmed from the fact that Fritz was very possessive. Hedy was a very independent woman, but Fritz didn't want her to act and tried to buy every copy of *Ecstasy* so that no one would be able to see her nude. He kept a close eye on Hedy and would not let her go where she wanted. Hedy was determined to escape. One night in 1937, she disguised herself as the maid, snuck out of the house, and did not stop until she got to Paris.

In 2003, the Boeing Company, which makes airplanes, put out a series of ads to attract scientists to their company. They featured a picture of Hedy with a title that read, "A moment of insight that helped secure the future." The ads didn't even note that Hedy was also an actress.

From there she traveled on to London, England, where she met Louis B. Mayer, a famous movie producer from the United States. Louis signed her to a contract with MGM Studios in Hollywood, and she was on her way to a new career in the United States. Hedy had left Europe just in time; World War II had begun.

Louis Mayer was very concerned with Hedy's image. She would not do another movie like *Ecstasy* for MGM. Her name, Hedwig Keisler, was also a problem for Louis. He thought she should change it to something that audiences would like better and that they wouldn't connect with *Ecstasy*. He was the one who gave her the name Hedy Lamarr, after another actress Barbara La Marr, whom Louis thought was very beautiful. With this new name, the movie studio could pretend that she had never acted in that other movie.

It wasn't long before Hedy was making movies in Hollywood and socializing with movie stars. Her first American movie, *Algiers*, was an instant hit and soon she was being invited to Hollywood parties where she met many famous people. At one gathering, she met George Antheil, a piano player who also wrote music for movies. While talking to George, she learned that he knew quite a lot about mechanical sound devices. She had never forgotten about the remote-controlled torpedo that Fritz had wanted to make and she immediately realized that George might be able to help her with an idea that she had. Before leaving the party, Hedy invited George to visit her home to further discuss her idea.

Hedy told George about her idea for a remote-controlled radio system that would allow signals to be transmitted without being detected, deciphered, or jammed. It was something she thought the U.S. government could use in the war against

Hedy Lamarr plays the role of Delilah in the 1949 Cecil B. DeMille film Samson and Delilah.

the Nazis. George was excited by her idea, which came to be known as "frequency hopping" and then later as "spread spectrum technology." He believed he could help her make it happen. George had a lot of experience with player pianos, which work using a roll of paper with holes punched in the pattern of the notes to be played. It allows the piano to play songs automatically, without the need for a person to play the keys. George realized he could create very quick "hops" between the radio frequencies in the same way that he created the notes on rolls for the player piano. He made paper rolls with eighty-eight frequencies (the same number of keys on a piano) for their invention.

In December 1940, George and Hedy sent a description of their invention to the National Inventors' Council. The chairman of the council, Charles F. Ketterling, who was also a research director at General Motors, suggested that they work on their idea further until they could patent it. Finally, on August 11, 1942, they received a patent. Hedy had remarried by this time and the name that appeared on the patent was Hedy Kiesler-Markey, so her participation in the invention went unnoticed. The patent was kept a secret since the communications system was being tested for use in the war. Even after the war was over, Hedy's role in the invention was not immediately recognized.

At the same time, Hedy continued to act in Hollywood movies. Her most successful movie was *Samson and Delilah*, released in 1949. Despite her success in Hollywood, Hedy still wanted to work on her invention. She even considered working for Ketterling at the National Inventors' Council, but she was persuaded to stay in Hollywood. Movie studios were always very concerned about the image of their actors. People would be surprised that such a beautiful woman also could have such innovative and important ideas, and Hedy's studio, MGM, did not want people to see Hedy as anything other than a beautiful actor. But Hedy wanted to contribute to the war effort in some way. She decided to sell war bonds, which raised money to pay for the war. People would invest their money in a savings bond and the government would be able to use the cash to pay for the needs of the soldiers and for military equipment. Since Hedy was so famous, she was able to raise a lot of money. She once raised $7 million at one event by selling war bonds.

In 2005, Hedy's birthday, November 9th, was officially declared to be "Inventors' Day" in Germany. The holiday is intended to remind us of all inventors—those who are well known and others like Hedy who haven't always been recognized for their work. It also is meant to encourage other people to pursue their own inventive ideas.

It was Hedy and George's dream to have their device used by the army in the war. They wanted to help in some way to defeat the Nazis. The navy turned down their communications device, because they thought that it was too big to put on a torpedo. George thought that it could be made smaller and believed the navy officials just lacked imagination. He thought that since the device worked something like a player piano, perhaps the navy officials imagined having to put a whole piano on their torpedoes!

The invention may not have been used in World War II, as its inventors had hoped, but it was, finally, put to use. In 1957, engineers at the Sylvania Electronics Systems Division in Buffalo, New York, took hold of the idea. Instead of piano rolls, they used electronics. Their version of Hedy's invention became commonly used in secure military communications. In 1959, George and Hedy's patent expired, which meant that someone else could use and patent the idea. In 1962, Sylvania's device was used on ships sent to Cuba. The idea behind their secret communications system, frequency hopping, went on to form the basis for other inventions. Today, this concept can be found behind the security systems in defense systems, satellites, cell phones, wireless Internet, and other devices.

Even after she stopped making films and was no longer a Hollywood star who was expected to live up to a certain image, she still did not tell anyone about her invention. Her biography, *Ecstasy and Me*, was published in 1965 and made no mention at all of her interest in inventing. In fact, she continued to deny for a very long time—even in the 1980s—that she was involved in inventing frequency hopping or a secret communications device. Eventually, however, the truth came out and she began to receive the recognition she deserved. In 1997, Hedy and George received the Electronic Frontier Foundation (EFF) Pioneer Award. That same year, Hedy was awarded a BULBIE Gnass Spirit of Achievement Award. She was the first woman to receive this prize, known as the "Oscar of Invention."

Eventually Hedy left her life in Hollywood and moved to Florida. She died on January 9, 2000, at the age of eighty-five. Though Hedy's secret communications device was never used in the war against the Germans, as she had wanted, it is still considered a success. She was able to see people use her idea to make many other useful inventions and finally could admit that she had been both a beautiful woman *and* an innovative thinker.

Chapter 6

Gertrude Belle Elion

1918–1999

Sometimes, when you are trying to work out a problem, it is hard to think of a new way to look at it. A big part of being an inventor is being able to see a new way of doing things that no one has ever thought of before. Gertrude Elion was very good at this—and has forty-five patents to show for it! As a cancer researcher, her open mind, curious nature, and willingness to try new things, helped her to develop many new drugs that have helped people fight disease.

Gertrude Belle Elion was born on January 23, 1918, in Manhattan, New York. Her parents were both immigrants to America. Her father, Robert Elion, moved to New York from Lithuania when he was twelve years old. He had to work very hard to earn the money he needed to go to school to become a dentist. His hard work and dedication paid off. He was very successful and had many dentistry offices around the city. Gertrude's mother, Bertha Cohen, came to New York from Poland when she was fourteen. She, too, had worked very hard to support herself. She had lived with her sisters and worked as a seamstress, making clothes, while going to school to learn English. She married Robert when she was nineteen years old.

When Gertrude was three, her grandfather left his home in Russia and came to live with them in America. He was a watchmaker who loved to read and could speak many languages. He and Gertrude spent a lot of time together, walking in parks around the city and talking. In 1924, the Elion family grew again when Gertrude's brother Herbert was born. A few years later, they moved from Manhattan to the Bronx, another borough in New York.

Life for new immigrants can be difficult. For Gertrude's parents, education was very important to their new life in America. They always encouraged Gertrude in her studies and wanted her to stay in school, even though at the time this wasn't always seen as important for girls.

But Gertrude did not need to be convinced to stay in school. She was a very good student and showed an interest in all her subjects—from math and science to English. She loved to read. Her favorite books were about scientists, especially Marie Curie, whom Gertrude admired greatly. Marie Curie was a famous European scientist who discovered and studied the new chemical elements radium and polonium. She won two Nobel Prizes for her work in chemistry and physics.

Gertrude did so well in school that she was able to skip two grades. She was only twelve when she started high school and fifteen when she graduated. However, she did not have enough money to pay for college and she did not know what to study. Though her father had a successful career in dentistry, their family was not wealthy. In 1929, the New York Stock Exchange had crashed and Gertrude's father, who had many investments, had lost a lot of money. Fortunately for Gertrude, Hunter College, which was the women's branch of the City College of New York, was free and she was able to continue her studies there.

The answer to her second problem—what to study in school—came to Gertrude through very sad circumstances. In 1933, Gertrude's grandfather died of stomach cancer. For Gertrude, it was very difficult to see her grandfather, whom she loved so deeply, in so much pain. This experience inspired her to help find a cure for cancer so that other people would not have to suffer as her grandfather had.

Gertrude decided to study chemistry so that she could become a cancer researcher. Most of the women in her science classes wanted to be teachers or nurses. Not many women were encouraged to become scientists. However, Gertrude had one professor, Dr. Otis, who saw that some of his students were more serious about research and he wanted to help them. Dr. Otis arranged study groups in his home for the women in his classes who wanted to know more about scientific research. He gave them articles about physics so that they could learn and talk about new developments in the field. When teaching her own students later in life, Gertrude would remember the special care and interest that Dr. Otis took in his students' learning.

Not surprisingly, Gertrude continued to do well in school. She graduated in 1937 with a degree in chemistry. But this was a difficult time in the world. There were not many jobs and many people were very poor. It was especially hard for Gertrude to find a job because, at that time, science research was not something women usually did. Women were teachers, nurses, and secretaries, but not scientists. Gertrude knew what she wanted and she didn't give up. She applied for many jobs and tried not to get too frustrated by the rejection she faced. It was hard even to get an interview for a job, and when she did, the attitudes about women in science proved to be a big obstacle. In one interview, she was told that she could not be hired because she was too pretty and that she would distract the other scientists!

Being a scientist is the kind of job where you have to keep learning all the time. Many scientists have PhDs, which means they have gone to school for many years to learn and research their subject to the standards set by the university. Since Gertrude only had a bachelor's degree, the first step in a university education, she could not get a job as a scientist. In order to go back to school to get her PhD, she needed a job so that she could earn money to pay for her continuing education. When it seemed as though she would never find work as a scientist, she took an unpaid job at the New York Hospital School of Nurses, teaching nurses how to do laboratory work. Though she needed to make money, Gertrude wanted the experience of working in a lab. After three months, she was offered another job, this time in a real lab! She was not paid very much, but it was enough money to save for school. Little by little, Gertrude was making progress toward her dream of being a professional researcher.

Gertrude began taking classes at New York University toward a master's degree in chemistry. She worked while going to school—first as a secretary in a doctor's office, then as a public school teacher. It was hard to work and study at the same time, but in 1941, she received her master's degree. She was the only woman in her graduating class.

While at school, Gertrude met Leonard Canter, a statistics major at City College. They fell in love and planned to get married. Tragically, Leonard died unexpectedly of an infection in his heart. It was an illness that easily could have been cured with penicillin, an antibiotic that would be discovered only two years later. Gertrude was heartbroken. She would never find another partner like Leonard. But instead of being paralyzed by grief, Gertrude became more dedicated to her work and to creating new medicines to save people.

After finishing her master's degree, it was much easier for Gertrude to find a job. World War II had started and many scientists left their regular jobs to work on projects for the war. People were now more open to women filling non-traditional jobs to help out while the men were away. Gertrude worked in a lab at A&P, a grocery store company, where she tested jams, pickles, and other foods. She then worked at a pharmaceutical lab for Johnson & Johnson.

Finally, in 1944, Gertrude found a job that would interest her for a very long time. Her father had received a medicine at his dentistry office from a pharmaceutical company called Burroughs Wellcome, located just outside New York City. Knowing that his daughter was looking for a job, he suggested that Gertrude call up the company. When she did, Gertrude was pleasantly surprised. The receptionist told her she should come in for an interview.

When Gertrude arrived at Burroughs Wellcome for her interview she was pleased to see another woman in the lab. She thought this was a good sign. But the woman, Elvira Falco, thought Gertrude was dressed too nicely and wouldn't be willing to get her hands dirty in the lab. Elvira would later learn how wrong she was about Gertrude, and the two women would eventually become great friends.

World War II was a dark time in world history; however, it opened doors for many women who wanted to work. Gertrude wanted more than anything to work in a lab, but it wasn't until the war, that she was able to find a job in one. "War changed everything," she once said. "Whatever reservations there were about employing women in laboratories simply evaporated."

Gertrude was hired as an assistant to George Hitchings, a scientist who was known for his unusual research methods. Her job was to research purines, chemical compounds found in human cells. It was thought that purines might be used for cancer research. Gertrude had finally found her dream job—she was a cancer researcher!

Even though Gertrude was happy with her new job, she still wanted to continue her studies and get her PhD. She enrolled in New York University again, but this time the double load of working and going to school proved to be too much for her. She was faced with the choice of quitting her job or putting her studies on hold. Because she felt she was doing such important and satisfying work at Burroughs Wellcome, she decided to keep her job and stop going to school.

Gertrude and George worked together on many experiments and together they developed a unique way of conducting research, a method that is now commonly used, but then was quite unusual. In the past, researchers would test several chemical compounds to see if they were a cure for a particular disease or illness. Gertrude and George, however, focused on the chemical compound itself. They would examine variations of chemicals and try to figure out how they worked. Then, based on what they learned about the behaviors and properties of these chemicals, they could try to apply them to solve medical problems.

Gertrude had a lot of success with this method and, over her career, she created several new drugs that helped save many, many lives. One of the medicines she invented was Purinethol. In 1950, fifty percent of children with acute leukemia, a kind of cancer, would die from the disease. Though Purinethol couldn't cure the disease, it did slow it down, which gave doctors and the patients more time to fight it. Through further experiments, Gertrude found that Purinethol was even more effective when it was combined with other drugs.

When Gertrude and George Hitchings won the Nobel Prize, Burroughs Wellcome gave them $250,000 each to donate to charity. Gertrude gave her money to her old school, Hunter College, to assist students of chemistry and biochemistry.

By mixing Purinethol with these other drugs, eighty percent of childhood leukemia cases can be cured.

In 1957, Gertrude created another drug that would be useful in treating a variety of medical problems. She had been studying the drug, Imuran, for almost seven years to figure out how it worked. In England, another scientist, Roy Calne, had been working on organ transplants. He contacted Gertrude to ask if some of the drugs she'd been working on would help his transplant patients (who, at this time, were dogs!). Sometimes, after a transplant, the patient's body rejects the new, foreign organ, particularly if the person donating the organ is not related. Gertrude gave Roy a sample of Imuran and it reduced the occurrence of rejection. In 1959, Roy transplanted a foreign kidney into Lollipop, a puppy patient. With the help of Imuran, Lollipop's new kidney worked just fine. In 1961, this success was repeated with a transplant on unrelated humans. Imuran also was found to be successful in treating arthritis, lupus, anemia, and hepatitis.

Gertrude continued her work at Burroughs Wellcome and was promoted many times. Sometimes she worked with George on projects and sometimes she did her own research. As she gained more experience, younger scientists began to work for her. Gertrude was a very good teacher and enjoyed helping new scientists in their work. In 1967, George retired from Burroughs Wellcome and Gertrude took over his job as the head of the Department of Experimental Therapy. She was the first woman to lead a major research group.

Over the course of her career, Gertrude developed many new medicines—she owns forty-five patents in all. In

1969, when she was fifty-one, Gertrude finally got her PhD. She was awarded an honorary PhD from George Washington University. Honorary degrees are given to recognize a person's special achievements in their field of work. In the end, Gertrude got to keep her job *and* get a PhD!

In 1983, after almost forty years of work for Burroughs Wellcome, Gertrude retired from the lab, but that doesn't mean she slowed down. She still visited the lab to answer questions and help the other researchers. She also became a professor at two universities in North Carolina. Gertrude loved to teach and mentor young scientists.

On October 17, 1988, Gertrude received an unexpected call from a reporter who asked her how she felt about winning the Nobel Prize. This was news to Gertrude! She found out that she'd won the Nobel Prize along with George Hitchings for a series of drugs they had created. Though Gertrude never married or had a family of her own, she was very close to her nieces and nephews. She invited the whole family to the Nobel Prize ceremony in Stockholm, Sweden.

Gertrude passed away on February 21, 1999, at the age of eighty-one. She had gained a lot of recognition for her work as a creator of life-saving drugs. Although she had wanted to be a researcher since she was fifteen years old, she had never been motivated by fame or money. She just wanted to help people. No matter how many awards she won, Gertrude always valued the gratitude of the people she helped more than anything. People from all over wrote to let her know how thankful they were that she had invented drugs that helped save their lives. She may have struggled in the beginning to find a job where she was allowed to explore her ideas, but in the end Gertrude was able to prove her intelligence and creativity, and help many people have longer and healthier lives.

Chapter 7

Stephanie Kwolek

1923–

Curiosity is an essential ingredient to invention. With curiosity—a simple desire to see how something will turn out—some of the greatest discoveries in the world are made. Stephanie Kwolek had, from an early age, the inquisitiveness that would help her to one day invent something that would change the world.

Stephanie was born in New Kensington, Pennsylvania, in 1923. Her father, John Kwolek, was a naturalist and spent his career studying plants and the great outdoors. Stephanie spent many hours of her childhood exploring the woods and creeks around her Pennsylvania home with her father and brothers. With her father's help she brought leaves, seeds, flowers, and other samples from nature back to her scrapbook to be carefully catalogued and described. Although her father passed away when she was only 10 years old, he instilled in Stephanie a lifelong interest in science.

After her father died, Stephanie's mother, Nellie Zajdel Kwolek, began working to support the family. She worked in fashion and design, and from her Stephanie developed an interest in fabrics and sewing. She even thought she might become a fashion designer, but her mother told her that she might starve in the fashion industry because of her perfectionism. Thus steered back toward science, Stephanie continued her schooling and developed a love of chemistry and medicine that would shape her future.

Stephanie attended Margaret Morrison Carnegie College, which was a women's college at Carnegie Mellon University in nearby Pittsburgh. She graduated from the college in 1946 with a degree in chemistry. Stephanie had decided to attend medical school after college, but she lacked the money to continue her education right away. She decided to get a job to save some money for a few years. She soon got an interview for a research position with the DuPont Company in Buffalo, NY. Her interviewer was W. Hale Charch, who was a well-known scientist, renowned for his invention of a process that made cellophane waterproof. Stephanie was impressed to be around such a great mind, but she was hardly intimidated. During the interview Charch told Stephanie that he would let her know if she got the job in two weeks. Stephanie boldly and craftily asked him if there was any way he could tell her sooner because she was trying to decide about another job offer (there was in fact no other job offer). Church called his secretary and asked her to write Stephanie a formal offer of employment right then and there. Stephanie strongly felt that it was her strength and assertiveness, as well as her excellent skills as a chemist, that turned the decision in her favor.

Although Stephanie had planned to only stay a few years, she found her work at DuPont far too interesting to leave. She decided not to go to medical school, but to have a career in chemistry. It was a decision that would change the rest of her life. She began working as a chemist at the DuPont textile fabrics laboratory in Buffalo. Working there reminded her of her early love of fabrics, which was now finally joined with her interest in research and chemistry. She worked with great determination at DuPont not only because she enjoyed the work, but because she didn't want to lose her laboratory position, as many women scientists did during World War II. Because women were thought of as more useful at home than in the lab, Stephanie was one of only a few female scientists who were still working by the end of the war.

Stephanie's hard work soon earned her advancement at DuPont. In 1950, she transferred to DuPont's Pioneering Research Laboratory in Wilmington, Delaware. Here she was quickly involved in many research projects involving new polymers. A polymer is a large molecule composed of repeating structural units. Plastics are a common example of polymers, but there are many more polymers that can be synthetically created in labs. One of the projects Stephanie worked on while at the research laboratory in Delaware involved the making of polymers that could not be melted. She helped create a polymer that would only start to fall apart at over 750 degrees Fahrenheit (400 degrees Celsius)!

In the 1960s, Stephanie was asked by DuPont to start working on a new generation of fibers that would be capable of withstanding some very extreme conditions. Stephanie had been working on a process called polymer condensation. This means creating long chains of molecules at very low temperatures. These long chain polymers formed liquid crystal while in a solution. This was something unique to those polymers at the time. For this reason, they were called crystalline polymers. The result of her experiments was a polymer solution that most researchers would have rejected. It was unlike any polymer solutions prepared at the time. It was fluid and cloudy, rather than thick and clear as most polymers up till then. In fact, the technician, working with the equipment needed to make the polymer solution into a finished product, didn't even want to run it through the machine. He thought it would break the expensive lab equipment. But Stephanie had a hunch it would work. She insisted on running the solution, and the results were astonishing. The synthetic fibers created were stiffer and stronger than any previously created.

The DuPont Pioneering Lab immediately went to work to market Stephanie's creation. These crystalline polymers created a product with the potential for many applications. DuPont called the substance Kevlar and began selling it in 1971. Kevlar is five times stronger than steel, but much less dense. It does not rust or corrode and is very lightweight and easy to carry around. Kevlar is used all over the world in tires and brake pads, fiberoptic cables, and even in the shells of spacecrafts. It is used to make cables to hold up enormous suspension bridges. It is also used to make sporting goods like ski equipment, camping gear, canoes, parachutes, and safety helmets.

However, perhaps the most well-known use of Kevlar is in the construction of a type of body armor known as bulletproof vests. When the bullet from a gun strikes the body armor, it is effectively caught up in a web of extremely strong polymer fibers. These synthetic polymers absorb the force of the bullet and disperse the energy from the impact, so that the full force

A Marine unpacks a Kevlar blanket used to protect the gunner of a TOW antitank missile system during a Weapons and Tactics Instructor Course at the Yuma Proving Ground in Yuma, Arizona.

of it doesn't all strike in one place. The vest has many layers, so the energy of the bullet is continually dispersed until the bullet is slowed down and eventually stopped. The vests are designed to be worn short term by police officers in situations where they might come under fire. Many police officers owe their lives to Stephanie for her world-changing invention.

The magnitude of Stephanie's creation has not been lost on the scientific community. She has received numerous awards for her invention. This includes being inducted into the National Inventors Hall of Fame in 1995. At the time, she was only the fourth member inducted out of a total of 113 members. In 1996, she went on to receive the National Medal of Technology. Then in the following year, she won the Perkin Medal, presented by the American Section of the Society of Chemical Industry. Both of these honors were rarely bestowed on female scientists. In 1999, Stephanie won the Lemelson-MIT Lifetime Achievement Award, which is given out to great inventors who create technological advances that make the world a better place and solve real-world problems.

Stephanie has always focused on hard work and determination, and never on the difficulties of being a woman in a male-dominated field. She wants to help other young women in science achieve their goals and has served as a mentor to young female scientists over the years. She has also worked in programs that introduce young children to science. Stephanie once wrote a paper called "The Nylon Rope Trick" that explains how to demonstrate condensation polymerization in a beaker at room temperature. This demonstration is now common in classrooms all over the country.

Stephanie continued to lead the way in polymer research at DuPont's Pioneering Lab until her retirement in 1986. During her forty years as a research scientist, she was the recipient of seventeen U.S. patents for her life's work. Stephanie continues to consult part-time for DuPont, where she is greatly respected for her keen scientific knowledge and insight. She also lectures around the country about her life's work and inventions. From a lifetime of following her scientific curiosity, Stephanie truly believes in the power of discovery and of following your instincts. As she says, "I love making discoveries. Generally, if things don't work out, I don't just throw them out, I struggle over them, to try and see if there's something there . . . You have to be inquisitive about things. You have to have an open mind." Through the power of curiosity and an open mind, Stephanie truly achieved something great.

Chapter 8

Bette Nesmith Graham

1924–1980

For Bette Nesmith Graham, the most important thing in life was to be able to live up to her full potential. She believed that every person has something to contribute and when they are encouraged and allowed to do so, great things can happen. Bette's invention may seem like a small thing, but it helped countless women in their jobs and allowed her to create a company where everyone was valued.

Bette was born Bette Claire McMurray on March 23, 1924, in Dallas, Texas. She came from a hardworking family that had a lot of experience in business. Her father, Jesse, worked in the wholesale auto business, and her great-grandfather, John Darby, founded Wesleyan College, one of the first women's colleges in the United States. But it was her mother, Christine, who probably had the biggest influence on Bette. Christine was an artist and a businesswoman. She learned how to knit from a friend and then went on to open her own store where she taught needlework and sold her own crafts and knitting supplies. At the time, it was a very unusual thing for a woman to run her own business. Bette, who noticed her mother's bold approach to life, would later take a simple solution to a problem at work and turn it into a successful, multimillion-dollar enterprise.

From a young age, it was obvious that Bette had inherited her mother's independent spirit. Referred to by her family as strong-willed and determined to do her own thing, Bette found that her teachers at school did not have such a positive view of her attitude. They called her stubborn and a troublemaker. Bette left school at seventeen and applied for a secretarial job at a law firm. She didn't know how to type, which was a large part of the job, but her charm and personality convinced them to hire her despite her lack of skills. The firm she worked for sent her to secretarial school, while at night she earned her high-school diploma.

On December 7, 1941, Pearl Harbor was bombed and the U.S. went to war with Japan. It was around this time that Bette met and married Warren Nesmith, an Army National Guardsman. When Warren had to leave to fight in the war, Bette was pregnant. Their son, Michael, was born on December 30, 1943. Like other soldiers, Warren was away from his family for several years, so Bette had to raise Michael alone. She continued to work as a secretary and did the best she could. Three years later, when the war was over, Warren finally returned home. But things were different between Warren and Bette. Too much had changed and they divorced a year later.

Bette kept her secretarial job and continued to look after her son. She was eventually promoted to executive secretary for the chairman of the Texas Bank & Trust in Dallas. This was a very high position for a woman to have in a company at that time. There was only one problem for Bette—her new typewriter. Before computers were invented, secretaries used typewriters to write letters and other documents. When Bette started out as a secretary, the typewriters she used were manual, which meant that you had to press very hard on the keys to type. As technology moved forward, electric typewriters were created and became more common in offices. These new machines were easier and faster, because you didn't have to press as hard on the keys to type, but it was also much easier to make mistakes. If you just brushed your finger against a key by mistake, it would type a letter, and fixing mistakes was a very messy process. Though Bette had been through secretarial school, typing was still not her strongest skill and she made many mistakes on the new electric machine.

Like her mother, Bette had an artistic side, and it was this talent that would lead to her invention. She noticed that painters never erased their mistakes; instead, they painted over them. This sparked an idea in her mind. She put some of her artist's paint in a bottle and took her watercolor brush along with her to work. The next time she made a mistake, she painted over it with white paint, put the paper back in the typewriter and typed over it. It became her secret trick and for five years, no one noticed what she was doing.

It was hard to keep it a secret forever, though, and soon the other secretaries were asking for her magic paint to help them with their work. She began to make up little bottles to sell to the other secretaries. When Bette first had her idea, she didn't think it would turn into a business and become her full-time career. She just needed to solve a problem she had at work. It wasn't until an office supply dealer asked her why she didn't sell the new product that Bette began to ponder the idea of starting her own business. To do that, though, she had to do a lot more work. She quickly discovered that it wasn't enough to just have a product that people wanted to buy.

First, Bette needed to improve her invention, which she originally called Mistake Out. Her first recipe took too long to dry. She researched the formula for the kind of paint she used, called tempera, with the help of a chemistry teacher at her son's school. Next, she learned how to make and mix paint from someone at a paint company. Finally, she took all that she'd read and been taught, and headed into the kitchen. Using her blender to mix the paint, she worked on the formula, testing many different combinations of ingredients. Finally, Bette found a recipe that made a type of paint that was the right color and that would dry quickly.

By 1957, Bette had moved on to a new job at IBM. She now had enough confidence in her product, which she called Liquid Paper, to market it to people other than her secretarial friends. She approached IBM and asked them if they would like to market her invention. IBM thought she could improve Liquid Paper even more and asked her to come back to them when it was perfected. This was disappointing, but Bette was not discouraged. Instead, she decided to market the product herself. It was a slow process, but by the end of her first year in business, Bette was selling 100 bottles each month. She had so many orders that she had to move the business from her kitchen to her garage. She still worked as a secretary during the day, so it was a lot of work to run her business on the side. Her son, Michael, and some of his friends helped by filling up the bottles. Soon, even the garage was not big enough for her company. Bette bought a shed to put in her backyard specifically for making and storing Liquid Paper.

Bette's business got a boost in 1958 when Liquid Paper was featured in a national office supply magazine called *The Office*. When they saw the

Bette's success with her invention still benefits many people—the women she helps through her foundations, her employees, and her son, Michael. Michael Nesmith was in The Monkees, a popular band who had their own TV show in the 1960s.

> Even though Bette's invention brought her a lot of money, she defined success in a very different way: "It is the ability to see a right idea in spite of the fact that others do not, and to cling to it in the face of discouragement and self-mistrust."
> — Bette Nesmith Graham

article, General Electric placed a large order. Bette now had so much to do that she found it hard to focus on her secretarial work. She was reluctant to quit her regular job, though, in case her new business didn't work out. One day, tired from working all night filling orders for Liquid Paper, Bette signed her own company's name at the bottom of a letter for her boss at IBM. She was fired for her mistake, but this meant she could now concentrate on her own business. Although her business was growing, she still wasn't making enough money from the business alone. She got a part-time job. With the money she made, she hired a chemist to help her perfect the formula for Liquid Paper. Slowly, what had begun as a side project was turning into Bette's real career.

Bette kept dividing her time between her part-time job and her Liquid Paper business until 1962, when she married Robert Graham, a frozen food salesman. With his extra support, she was able to turn Liquid Paper into a true success. By 1968, the company had its own headquarters and production plant, producing 10,000 bottles of Liquid Paper a day. Sales were booming; the company drew in more than $1 million a year. Now thousands of people, not just a few secretaries, were using Liquid Paper.

Over the next decade, the company continued to grow and prosper. By 1975, Bette had 200 employees, and Liquid Paper was being sold in thirty-one countries around the world. Bette was a very caring and supportive boss. She believed that it was important for people to be able to discover and use their true talents. Everyone in her company, from the secretaries to the vice-president, was valued for the work that they did. She also set up a day care and a library in the production plant to help her employees.

For Bette, 1975 was a year of change. She divorced Robert and stopped working at the Liquid Paper company, though she continued to own it. Instead, she decided to devote her time to charity work, and over the next couple of years, she established two foundations, the Gihon Foundation and the Bette Claire McMurray Foundation. The Gihon Foundation was created to help people learn about women artists. The Bette Claire McMurray Foundation gives money to women's and arts' groups, such as the Girls Club of America, the American Film Institute, and the National Women's Education Fund.

In 1979, Bette sold her company to the Gillette Corporation for $47.5 million. The little idea she had to help her secretarial career had propelled her into the life of a successful businesswoman. Through it all, she followed her own sense of direction. Six months after she sold her company, on May 12, 1980, Bette passed away at the age of fifty-six. She left half of her fortune to her son and the other half to her foundations. Bette had managed to build a business that today sells its products all over the world, yet she did not believe that this equaled true success. For Bette, real success was achieved when a person was able to truly express his or her own individuality. To be free to be unique and follow her own ideas and her own dreams was the true sign for Bette that she had achieved something great.

Bette's Liquid Paper.

Chapter 9

Patricia Bath

1942–

It's hard to be the first at anything. How do you even know that what you want to accomplish is even possible? Patricia Bath has been the first to achieve many things in her field. She was lucky enough to have parents who encouraged her to work hard in school and who taught her that she could do anything she wanted. Patricia has used her strong faith in her own abilities to help other people as well. Her belief that everyone deserves the same quality of medical care, regardless of where they were born or how much money they have, has improved the lives of people in many parts of the world.

Patricia Bath was born in Harlem, New York, on November 4, 1942. At that time, Harlem was a neighborhood that some people thought of as poor and dangerous. Patricia never saw it that way. She grew up in a loving home and has many happy memories of her childhood. Patricia believed that she could do anything and go anywhere if she worked hard in school.

Her father, Rupert, was born in Trinidad and was originally a merchant seaman traveling the world while working on ships. When he moved to New York City, he took a job as a motorman for the city's subway. He was the first Black man in New York to have that job. Rupert also was very involved in the community and he wrote a column for a newspaper called the *Amsterdam News*. Patricia's mother, Gladys, was born in America. Her ancestors were African slaves and Cherokee Native Americans. Gladys worked very hard at home, and also had a job as a domestic (a maid), cleaning other people's houses. She always encouraged Patricia to read. Her parents worked very hard so that Patricia could go to university. They wanted her to have the best possible education.

Patricia did not disappoint them. She loved school and did very well from the beginning. She especially liked biology and even spent extra time in the lab after school, working on projects. From an early age, Patricia matched her love for science with a sincere wish to help people. When she was young, she had learned about Albert Schweitzer, a famous doctor who traveled to Africa. He treated people who otherwise would not have had access to medicine or doctors. Patricia was inspired by his work and wanted to help others in the same way.

At Charles Evans Hughes High School, Patricia was the editor of the school science paper and won many science awards. When she was just sixteen, she won the National Science Foundation Fellowship, a summer program that gave her the opportunity to study cancer research at the Yeshiva Albert Einstein College of Medicine in New York. While studying at Yeshiva, she designed a math equation to predict cell growth. One of her teachers, Dr. Robert O. Bernard, included her formula in a paper he presented at an international conference the next year, and it attracted national media attention.

Patricia advanced very quickly in her classes, finishing high school in only two and a half years. In 1960, when she was eighteen, she won an award from *Mademoiselle*, a women's magazine, in recognition of her achievements in science and the promise she showed for the future.

With so much success early in her life, it seemed obvious that Patricia would continue her education in the sciences at university. She went on to study chemistry and physics at Hunter College in New York City. After four years, she graduated with a bachelor's degree. But Patricia felt she needed to continue her studies even further. She moved to Washington, DC, to go to medical school at Howard University. This turned out to be a very important experience. She met many helpful people with more experience who could help to guide her, and these mentors included Dr. LaSalle, Dr. Leffall Jr., and Dr. Lois A. Young. Seeing successful, intelligent Black professors helped Patricia believe that she also could excel in her studies and go on to do great things.

It was during medical school that Patricia took her first trip outside of the United States. One summer, she worked in Yugoslavia on a research project. This was her first opportunity to see the quality of health and medicine in another country. The next summer, she worked as a medical coordinator for the Poor People's Campaign in the U.S. They marched in Washington to demand that the rights of all people, regardless of their wealth, be recognized and valued by the government. So many people showed up to demonstrate that they had to set up a camp near the Lincoln Memorial. It was Patricia's job to make sure that all the demonstrators in the camp were healthy and that the conditions in the camp were clean and safe.

In 1968, Patricia graduated from Howard University and became a doctor. She moved back to her old neighborhood of Harlem in New York. To be a doctor, you have to do more than just go to school—you also have to work as an intern in a hospital with other doctors to get real-life experience. Patricia interned at Harlem Hospital.

During her time at the hospital, Patricia treated many Black patients. She noticed that almost fifty percent of them were blind or had some problems seeing properly. She didn't know why so many had eye problems, but she realized that it was something that needed to be addressed.

Patricia Bath no doubt spent many hours studying and researching in the Founders Library of Howard University (above). Bath graduated from Howard's medical school in 1968.

Patricia decided to go back to school. She stayed in New York and went to Columbia University. Her area of study was ophthalmology, the branch of medicine that focuses on treating eye diseases. As part of her studies, she did another internship, this time at the Columbia Eye Clinic. There, a smaller number of the patients she treated were Black. Most were white, and Patricia noticed that the white patients did not have the same rates of blindness or other vision problems as her Black patients at the Harlem Hospital. It made her curious as to why there should be a difference, so she started to study the rates of blindness of white and Black people in the United States. She found that, at the time, Black people had almost double the rate of blindness compared to white people. Patricia believed that this was mostly because Black people did not have the same access to eye care as the white people in America. That realization would shape much of her work from that point onward.

Patricia knew something had to be done to give everyone the same level of eye care. She created something called community ophthalmology, which now is studied and practiced in much of the world. Community ophthalmology trains volunteers in eye care. The volunteers visit community centers to test seniors and children for eye problems. By going out to the centers, many people who would otherwise not be able to go to an eye doctor have the chance to get proper care. This can prevent many serious problems from occurring later on. It can be especially important for children. Children who have untreated

Patricia has been honored many times for her exceptional work in the field of eye health: in 1989, she was elected to the Hall of Fame of Hunter College of the City University of New York; in 1993, she was named Howard University Pioneer in Academic Medicine; and in 1995, she received the National Association for the Advancement of Colored People (NAACP) Black Woman of Achievement Award.

eye problems may have difficulties in school. If they can't see the blackboard, for example, they can get headaches or have problems focusing on their work. Often, they don't realize that the difficulties they have in school are due to poor eyesight. By testing the children early and giving eyeglasses to the ones who need them, the volunteers are really helping the children with their education and lives, not just with the health of their eyes.

In 1970, Patricia went to New York University to continue her training as an ophthalmologist. In 1972, she had a daughter, Eraka. Now Patricia had to balance her academic and research work with being a mom. It was hard work, but Patricia remained a dedicated student. She stayed in school and completed postgraduate work that focused on particular types of eye transplants and surgery for inserting a lens in a scarred eye. In 1973, she became the first Black resident in her field.

Dr. Patricia Bath watches over President Barack Obama's shoulder as he signs a Presidential Memorandum on Scientific Integrity.

In 1993, Patricia retired from the UCLA Medical Center, but she hasn't stopped working altogether. She was elected to the Center's honorary medical staff (the first woman, again) and she continues to work to improve eye health worldwide. Patricia encourages telemedicine, which uses communications devices like the Internet to help people in remote or underprivileged areas get access to medical treatments.

In 1974, Patricia moved to Los Angeles where she took on a job as assistant professor at Charles R. Drew University and worked at Martin Luther King Jr. General Hospital. She was as committed to her students as she was to her patients. The director of her department at Charles Drew University, Dr. Timothy Scott, along with Patricia and others, helped to set up an ophthalmology residency training program. Patricia believed that this was an important step in increasing the number of Black and other minority ophthalmologists in the United States. Perhaps being inspired by the Black doctors at Howard University in her early years made her want to give other students the same chance. Later, she was promoted to chair of the residency program, becoming the first woman to hold such a job. In 1975, Patricia broke new ground again when she became the first Black woman surgeon at the UCLA Medical Center and the first woman to be on the faculty of the UCLA Jules Stein Eye Institute.

In 1976, Patricia and three other doctors founded the American Institute for the Prevention of Blindness (AIPB). They believed that eyesight is a basic human right. This means that everyone should have basic eye care, no matter where he or she lives or how much money he or she has. Today the AIPB works in many countries to try to ensure that people have equal access to eye health. To do this, the AIPB donates eye drops, vitamin A supplements, and vaccines that could help prevent blindness.

Patricia worked as the director of the AIPB. She traveled to countries such as England, France, Nigeria, Thailand, China, Tanzania, Pakistan, and Yugoslavia, to speak about the importance of eye health and share her medical techniques with other doctors.

It was also in 1976 that Patricia had the idea for her invention, the Laserphaco Probe, which would change the way ophthalmologists perform cataract surgery. A cataract is a cloudiness on the lens of the eye that makes it hard for a person to see. If the cataract is not treated, the person may go blind. A cataract can form for many different reasons—because of a disease (such as diabetes, for instance), or long-term exposure to ultraviolet rays (like those of the sun), or just due to aging. The Laserphaco Probe is used to remove cataracts so that a new eye lens can be inserted. Before Patricia's invention, doctors had to use traditional surgery to remove cataracts. It was a much more difficult technique. Patricia's laser has made removing cataracts easier, safer, and more accurate. Many people who had vision problems for several years can have clear eyesight again due to her invention.

Initially, many people told Patricia that her idea of using a laser for eye surgery was impossible. UCLA did not have the lasers that she needed for her invention because most of the laser technology in the United States at that time was being used for military purposes. Therefore, when she designed her laser probe, she had to test it in Germany.

Like other inventors, once Patricia had developed her invention, she had to patent it. But the Laserphaco Probe was made up of many original ideas and Patricia had to file a patent for each one. It was a long and difficult process. At first, she hired lawyers to help her. After nine years, when she still did not have the patents, Patricia decided to learn how

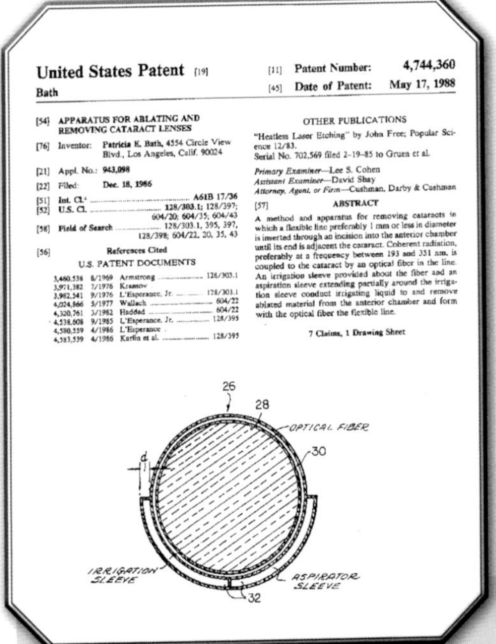

United States Patent [19]
Bath

[11] **Patent Number:** 4,744,360
[45] **Date of Patent:** May 17, 1988

[54] APPARATUS FOR ABLATING AND REMOVING CATARACT LENSES

[76] Inventor: **Patricia E. Bath**, 4554 Circle View Blvd., Los Angeles, Calif. 90024

[21] Appl. No.: **943,098**

[22] Filed: **Dec. 18, 1986**

[51] **Int. Cl.**[4] **A61B 17/36**
[52] **U.S. Cl.** **128/303.1**; 128/397; 604/20; 604/35; 604/43
[58] **Field of Search** 128/303.1, 395, 397, 128/398; 604/22, 20, 35, 43

[56] **References Cited**

U.S. PATENT DOCUMENTS

3,460,538	8/1969	Armstrong	128/303.1
3,971,382	7/1976	Krasnov	
3,982,541	9/1976	L'Esperance, Jr.	128/303.1
4,024,866	5/1977	Wallach	604/22
4,320,761	3/1982	Haddad	604/22
4,538,608	9/1985	L'Esperance, Jr.	128/395
4,580,559	4/1986	L'Esperance	
4,583,539	4/1986	Karlin et al.	128/395

OTHER PUBLICATIONS

"Heatless Laser Etching" by John Free; Popular Science 12/83.
Serial No. 702,569 filed 2-19-85 to Gruen et al.

Primary Examiner—Lee S. Cohen
Assistant Examiner—David Shay
Attorney, Agent, or Firm—Cushman, Darby & Cushman

[57] **ABSTRACT**

A method and apparatus for removing cataracts in which a flexible line preferably 1 mm or less in diameter is inserted through an incision into the anterior chamber until its end is adjacent the cataract. Coherent radiation, preferably at a frequency between 193 and 351 nm, is coupled to the cataract by an optical fiber in the line. An irrigation sleeve provided about the fiber and an aspiration sleeve extending partially around the irrigation sleeve conduct irrigating liquid to and remove ablated material from the anterior chamber and form with the optical fiber the flexible line.

7 Claims, 1 Drawing Sheet

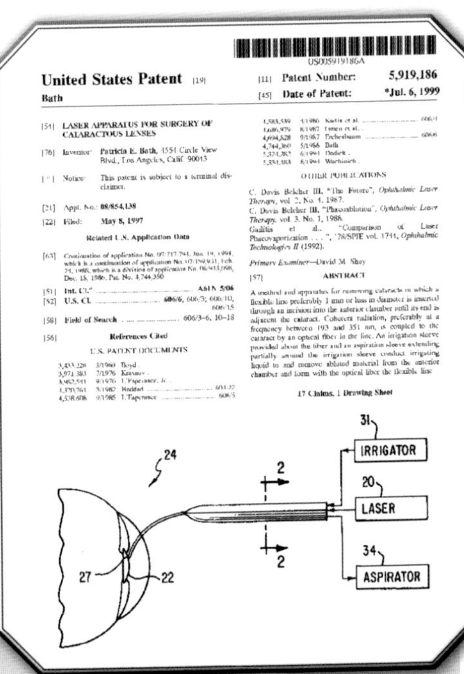

US005919186A

United States Patent [19]
Bath

[11] **Patent Number:** 5,919,186
[45] **Date of Patent:** *Jul. 6, 1999

[54] LASER APPARATUS FOR SURGERY OF CATARACTOUS LENSES

[76] Inventor: **Patricia E. Bath**, 4554 Circle View Blvd., Los Angeles, Calif. 90043

[*] Notice: This patent is subject to a terminal disclaimer.

[21] Appl. No.: **08/854,138**

[22] Filed: **May 8, 1997**

Related U.S. Application Data

[63] Continuation of application No. 07/717,794, Jun. 19, 1991, which is a continuation of application No. 07/159,931, Feb. 24, 1988, which is a division of application No. 06/943,098, Dec. 18, 1986, Pat. No. 4,744,360

[51] **Int. Cl.**[6] **A61N 5/06**
[52] **U.S. Cl.** **606/6**; 606/3; 606/10, 606/15
[58] **Field of Search** 606/3–6, 10–18

[56] **References Cited**

U.S. PATENT DOCUMENTS

3,433,226	3/1969	Boyd	
3,971,383	7/1976	Krasnov	
3,982,541	9/1976	L'Esperance, Jr.	
4,320,761	3/1982	Haddad	604/22
4,538,608	9/1985	L'Esperance	606/5
4,583,539	4/1986	Karlin et al.	606/4
4,686,979	8/1987	Gruen et al.	
4,694,828	9/1987	Eichenbaum	606/6
4,744,360	5/1988	Bath	
5,324,282	6/1994	Dodick	
5,334,183	8/1994	Wuchinich	

OTHER PUBLICATIONS

C. Davis Belcher III, "The Future", *Ophthalmic Laser Therapy*, vol. 2, No. 4, 1987.
C. Davis Belcher III, "Phacoablation", *Ophthalmic Laser Therapy*, vol. 3, No. 1, 1988.
Gailitis et al., "Comparison of Laser Phacovaporization . . . ", '78/SPIE vol. 1644, *Ophthalmic Technologies II* (1992).

Primary Examiner—David M. Shay

[57] **ABSTRACT**

A method and apparatus for removing cataracts in which a flexible line preferably 1 mm or less in diameter is inserted through an incision into the anterior chamber until its end is adjacent the cataract. Coherent radiation, preferably at a frequency between 193 and 351 nm, is coupled to the cataract by an optical fiber in the line. An irrigation sleeve provided about the fiber and an aspiration sleeve extending partially around the irrigation sleeve conduct irrigating liquid to and remove ablated material from the anterior chamber and form with the optical fiber the flexible line.

17 Claims, 1 Drawing Sheet

This diagram is part of Dr. Patricia Bath's patent application for her Laserphaco Probe, an apparatus designed to remove cataracts via laser surgery.

to file for patents herself. The process took a few years. In the meantime, Patricia kept working and saw the same success in her professional life as she had in school. In 1977, she founded and served as director of the Ophthalmic Assistant Training Program of the UCLA Department of Ophthalmology, which was the first program of its kind in California. She continued to teach at UCLA, first as an assistant professor of ophthalmology in 1979, then as an associate professor (which is a higher position). In 1983, she was promoted again to chair of the Ophthalmology Residency Training Program, which made her the first woman in the country to hold a position like that.

In 1988, Patricia finally received her first patent, making her the first Black woman doctor to receive a patent for a medical invention. It seems that no matter what Patricia set out to do, she was always a trailblazer.

Patricia's invention is only part of her contribution. She has helped to improve eye health for people in many parts of the world and also works as an educator to help students learn about ophthalmology. Underlying all of her work is the belief that everyone can achieve success in their chosen fields, no matter where they come from or how wealthy they are. Through her work for AIPB, she has met other people in her field, learned from them and passed on her own knowledge and experience. She has lectured and performed surgery in many countries. In 1981, Patricia and her daughter traveled to many countries around the world to see, firsthand, the kinds of health services people receive in different countries. In the future, Patricia would like to establish a World Eye Institute to prevent, treat, and cure blindness. Making sure that everyone has access to proper eye care has become a lifelong goal for Patricia, and she's not done yet.

Chapter 10

Wendy Murphy

1946–

Imagination is critical to inventing. With our imaginations we can dream of things that don't yet exist and see how we can make them real. Wendy Murphy has always had an active imagination, even when she was just a young girl. She never expected, however, that her creative mind would change her life. After seeing a short news clip on television, Wendy had an idea that hospitals around the world would later come to use to save lives.

Wendy was born in Barrie, Ontario, on November 29, 1946. Her father, James Reuben Manship, worked for the military, so the family moved almost every two years. For many people, this would have been a very difficult thing to do, but it seemed to work for this family. It taught Wendy how to adapt to new situations, like catching up to her new class and meeting new people. Wendy's mother, Helen Kilroy, stayed at home to raise Wendy and her two younger sisters, Mary Lynn and Catherine.

Wendy's parents were very supportive and encouraging. They taught the girls always to be open to new ideas and experiences in order to recognize opportunities when they came along. Wendy's dad in particular told her that she could do anything she wanted as long as she was willing to work hard. At the time, attitudes toward women were still very limiting. Women were taught that there were only certain things they could do, but Wendy's dad taught her that she had the same rights as everyone else.

Wendy had a naturally curious, active, and imaginative mind. When she listened to the teacher in class describe a problem or an idea, her mind would spin off with a million interesting thoughts about it.

After high school, Wendy decided to move to Toronto to take an X-ray technician training course at the Toronto General Hospital. She was interested in medicine but didn't want to do certain things that nurses do, like giving needles. Her cousin was a radiologist and told her about this new field of medicine. Wendy thought it sounded like an interesting and promising job.

From 1965 to 1967, Wendy trained at the hospital and did well in the program. After her training, she wanted to take a tour of Europe, but her plans changed when she took a job at the Toronto Hospital for Sick Children. She stayed there for the next twenty-three years!

In 1976, while Wendy was taking time off from work after the birth of her first son, Scott, a friend who worked in a dental lab doing special facial X-rays asked Wendy to fill in for her while she was on vacation. Wendy agreed to do it. She worked doing facial X-rays until she heard about another opportunity at the hospital. This position required working with a new way to examine patients using sound waves called ultrasound. She would be working in the neonatal intensive care unit, which is an area of the hospital that takes care of babies who are sick or who were born too early. Wendy always liked trying new things, so she was interested. Even though the job was to last for only one year and the pay was low, she took it. For Wendy, this was another opportunity to learn something new. The knowledge she gained about the needs of babies in intensive care would help her develop her invention in the future. Her friends who worked in the X-ray department thought she was crazy to take on this new job. But at the end of the first year, her contract was extended and she got a pay raise. Now some of the other X-ray technicians wanted her job!

While working on her first invention, the baby stretcher, a light bulb turned on in Wendy's imagination—and it happened during a blackout. When the power went out in her home, she realized that in the dark there would be no way to tell with a flashlight where the tops of the pockets were. How could the nurses or rescue workers make sure the babies didn't fall out? It was then that Wendy had the idea to place reflective tape in the shape of an arrow on each pocket to show which side was up.

The inspiration for Wendy's invention came in 1985. She was watching TV when she saw news coverage of a devastating earthquake that had taken place in Mexico City. The news showed rescuers working at a hospital that had collapsed. Babies in their incubators had survived and had to be taken out of the rubble. (An incubator is a heated crib that keeps newborn babies warm.) Wendy saw rescuers put the babies on a stretcher made for adults. They had no way to keep the little ones secure on the stretcher so they had to hold the babies down while carrying the stretcher. Wendy was surprised to see that the rescuers didn't have a stretcher designed to get the babies to safety faster. Her imagination was sparked—she thought there must be a better way, and she began to make some drawings of a stretcher made just for babies. She came up with a design but didn't know how to develop it.

Then, in 1987 the Hospital for Sick Children in Toronto, where Wendy worked, had a fire in a lab a few floors below the neonatal intensive care floor. The firefighters tried to put out the fire, but it wasn't going well. They came up to Wendy's floor and told her that soon they might have to evacuate the babies. Luckily, they managed to put out the fire and did not have to move the babies after all. But the next day, everyone realized that they had to find a way to evacuate the babies if there was ever another emergency. The Chief of Neonatology, Dr. Smith, put together an emergency planning committee and Wendy agreed to join. She told the committee about her design for a baby stretcher, thinking that someone else would be able to use her idea and do something with it. She brought her drawings and a stretcher frame into the discussion to explain that each stretcher would have three pockets; each pocket could hold two babies. Nurses or rescuers could transport six babies to safety on a single stretcher without having to hold the babies down while moving them. Dr. Smith ordered ten of these stretchers on the spot. Wendy was shocked. She had never thought about making the stretchers herself, but Dr. Smith insisted that Wendy was the only one who could do it.

Wendy's WEEVAC 6 stretcher has won many awards, including the Manning Innovation Award, the National Research Council of Canada 75th Anniversary Award for Outstanding Innovativeness in Medical Device Technology, and the Sir Joseph Flavelle Award for Technical Innovation. In 2006, it was listed as one of the Fifty Greatest Canadian Inventions by the Canadian Broadcasting Corporation.

For the next two years, Wendy worked on her invention. She had to find the right materials, the right frame, and the right people to sew the stretcher fabric. At the same time, she kept working at the hospital. It was hard for Wendy to work all day and then come home to work on her invention, but it was something she felt she had to do.

Wendy found a folding frame and figured out how to fasten on the fabric so that it would not come off by accident while the babies were being transported, but she still had to choose a fabric. Usually, stretchers are made with canvas, a type of heavy fabric. Wendy wasn't sure that she wanted to use canvas, so she looked at many samples to see what else might work. While looking through a book of samples, she came across a heavy silver material that often is used in pizza delivery bags to keep the pizzas warm, and is fire resistant. Wendy knew how important it was for babies to stay warm in their incubators, so this fabric seemed perfect. Now she had all the different parts for her invention and she began to put together her first order.

In 1989, she got her first patent for the stretcher, which she called the WEEVAC 6. She delivered her order to Dr. Smith, and the Hospital for Sick Children in Toronto became the first hospital to use WEEVAC stretchers. People at other hospitals quickly found out about Wendy's invention. In fact, many people were wondering why she hadn't called them up to tell them

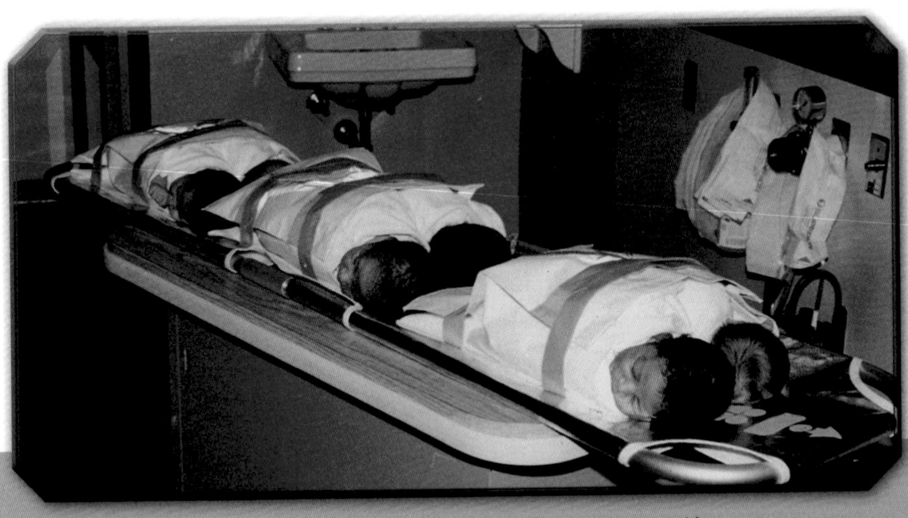

The WEEVAC 6 can transport up to six babies at one time.

Wendy's stretcher, named WEEVAC, can stand for three different things: "We evacuate," "we evacuate wee ones," or "Wendy's evacuation" stretcher.

about it! Wendy had not realized how much her stretcher was needed in hospitals all over the world.

Shortly after, Wendy went to a trade show for hospitals, where she talked to people about problems they had moving other kinds of patients, such as older people or people who could not leave their beds. Immediately, Wendy began making sketches for another kind of stretcher. These drawings later became the WEEVAC TC (which stands for thermal carpet), a stretcher that slides along the floor and down the stairs, making moving adult patients much easier.

In 1990, an unexpected event triggered a big change in Wendy's life. She was in her car when it was hit from behind, throwing her forward and leaving her with many painful injuries. It was hard for Wendy to keep working after the accident, so she took a break and focused on getting better. Three years later, in January 1993 as she was slowly recovering, she had a second, similar accident and in November of that year, she was hit from behind a third time! Wendy was so hurt that she knew she would never be able to go back to work at the hospital again.

Wendy had nothing left to do but focus on her business. It kept her going even when she was not feeling well. She kept selling the WEEVAC stretchers, but she also had several opportunities to make new products. The first one came when she got a call from the University of Alberta. The medical engineers at the hospital there were keenly interested in the material Wendy had chosen for the WEEVAC 6. They were designing a special type of incubator to be used when babies were moved to or from the hospital. They needed someone to design a cover for the transport incubator that would hold in as much heat as possible. It was clear that Wendy was the person for the job.

The engineers didn't know what the final incubator would look like or how big it would be, so Wendy had to start working without much information. She wondered how to make a cover that would have all the features that the nurses working with the babies wanted. Wendy called nurses at hospitals in Toronto and Edmonton to ask them what kinds of things they would like to have on this new cover. Eventually she designed a cover, with pockets on the sides and back and made of a material that would retain heat. When it was finally done, she wasn't sure it would fit on the incubator, but to her surprise it was a perfect match. Wendy had just successfully created the most energy-efficient incubator cover in the world!

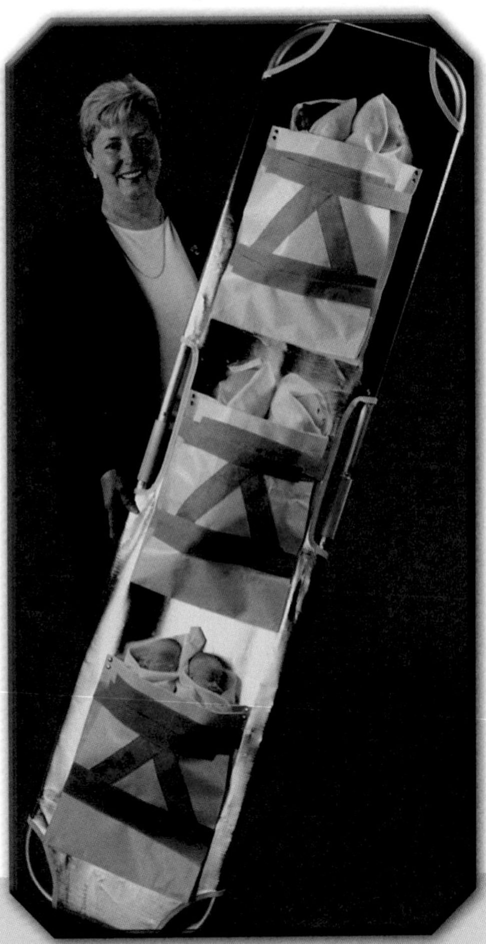

Using six dolls, Wendy Murphy demonstrates the WEEVAC stretcher that she invented.

Wendy assumed that this would be the only cover she would ever design, but word of her third invention got around. Some nurses at the University of Alberta wrote a paper on her incubator cover and it caught the eye of the equipment manager at British Columbia's Children's

"You can't look at anything as failing; everything is a learning experience. If you keep trying and keep enjoying what you do, you can't fail."
— Wendy Murphy

Hospital. The equipment manager thought it would be a useful thing for their transport team, which traveled throughout the province to bring babies to the hospital for treatment.

Even though they are very useful and help save babies' lives, Wendy didn't earn a lot of money on her incubator covers, but then, she hadn't created the covers to make money. She believes that the experience alone was worthwhile, and working on the covers helped her while she was recovering from her accidents.

In 1999, after undergoing many major surgeries to help correct the injuries she had sustained from her accidents, Wendy left Toronto to live in Deep River, a small town in Ontario where her sisters live. Wendy is able to run her business from Deep River since most of her orders come from the Internet. Her products are so well known and respected that she doesn't even have to make sales calls anymore. When Wendy first saw that news clip of the earthquake and wondered, "Isn't there a better way?" she couldn't have foreseen that the answer to that question would change her life. For Wendy, every day is a new experience because she never knows what opportunity will come her way or where her imagination will lead her.

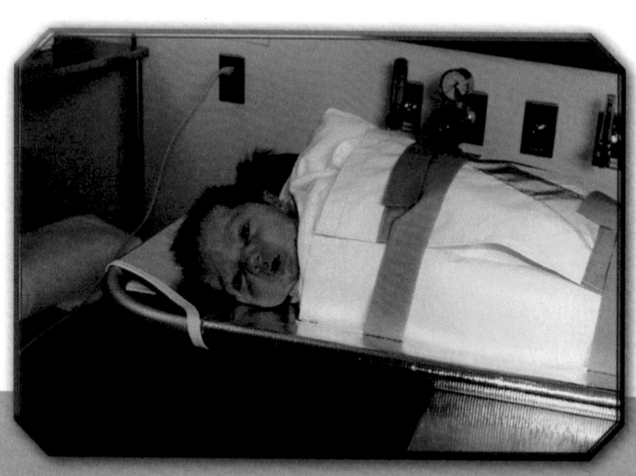

The WEEVAC stretcher up close.

Chapter 11

Laurie Tandrup

1956–

Life is full of unexpected twists and turns. The path we imagine for ourselves is often not the one we end up taking. This has certainly been true for Laurie Tandrup. She had never thought of herself as an inventor—she made her first invention for her sons in order to save a family trip from disaster, but when she saw how useful it was, she knew she had to share it with other people. Now Laurie runs her own successful business out of her home by selling a range of products she has designed herself. As Laurie's experiences show, sometimes good ideas result from strange circumstances. The key is to be flexible and positive, because you never know what adventures a surprise detour might bring.

Laurie Tandrup was born on August 12, 1956. She grew up in St. Albert, a small town outside of Edmonton, Alberta. Laurie is the second-oldest of five children. She has two brothers, Ted and Rick, and two sisters, Leslie and Michelle. Their mother, Nan, looked after the bustling household while their father, Kaj Eric, worked for the government as a surveyor. Eric also was a flying instructor, and when Laurie was a young girl, he would give her a plane ride for every "A" she got on her report card.

Life changed dramatically for Laurie when she was just seven years old. Her father died in a plane crash while he was teaching. Suddenly Laurie had to take on extra responsibilities at home and help raise her younger siblings. She still managed to indulge her love for books, however. Reading was something that helped her deal with all the difficult changes in her life.

When Laurie was just finishing Grade Seven, the family moved to Edmonton. Her mother remarried, but when that didn't work out, she decided to go back to school. Nan was an avid seamstress and became qualified to teach commercial sewing in special education classes.

Laurie also found new interests in Edmonton. She started taking classes at a local gymnastics club. When she was fourteen, she landed her first job, teaching the younger gymnastics students. Laurie's high school years were busy ones. She enjoyed track and field and wanted to be a physical education teacher. Since her family didn't have much money, she planned to work for a year after graduating from high school to save up enough for university.

Laurie's plan to go to university took a detour when she met a singer from Ireland and fell in love with him. She moved to Ireland where they were married in 1975. For the next four years, Laurie would follow her husband back and forth between Canada and Ireland many times. Each time, Laurie found jobs that would increase her experience with owning and running a business.

Back in Canada in 1979, Laurie began working for Canadian Laboratory Supplies, or CanLab. She stayed at CanLab for almost fifteen years, earning promotions until she was the operations manager for the local office. The company sold hospital supplies and Laurie managed the orders, inventory, and accounts, and learned how hospitals order and pay for their supplies. She had no idea at the time, but this job would help her in the future when she needed to sell her own inventions to hospitals.

Laurie's marriage did not last as long as her career at CanLab, and in 1980, she and her husband divorced. Through a friend from work, she met Colin. Laurie and Colin were married in 1983, and, in 1993, they had their first child, Kaj. When Laurie first held Kaj in the hospital, she immediately gave him the nickname "Snuglbud." It just seemed to suit this new addition to her family.

The next year brought a big change for Laurie. She was laid off from her job at Canadian Laboratory Supplies while she was pregnant with her second child. Erik was born in June 1995, and that summer, Laurie planned a family camping trip in Kelowna, British Columbia. A few weeks before the trip, she took the boys with her while shopping to buy supplies for the trip. Afterward, Laurie and her sons met her mother in the river valley for a walk before heading home. When they returned to the parking lot, they discovered that their car, with all of the camping supplies inside, had been stolen. Most important, Laurie had no way to get her sons home safely without their car seats. Laurie's insurance would cover the cost of the car, but not the car seats inside.

Still determined to go on the trip, she set about getting ready despite this setback. But her sons needed new car seats. Erik was just a small baby at the time and Laurie didn't want to buy another infant carrier since he would need a bigger seat within the year. So she decided to buy two bigger seats, one for each boy, and make some cushions to put into Erik's seat so he would fit properly and be safe. She designed a series of cushions to use on the trip—not just for the car seat, but also for changing Erik, supporting him in his highchair, and protecting him while he slept. To make sure that her cushions were safe for her son, Laurie asked her

Laurie Tandrup's sons, Kaj (left) and Erik (right), were the inspiration for her invention, the Travelbud car seat.

doctor for advice. Her doctor reassured her that the cushions were safe and the family set off on their trip. During their two weeks of camping, many people noticed Laurie's invention. They were curious about where she got her cushions, which seemed so useful. It was during this trip that Laurie realized her invention could help a lot of people with small babies who needed support.

By the time Laurie returned from her trip, she had decided to make her cushions available to other people. She enrolled in a government program, called self-employment assistance, that helps people who want to start their own businesses. The administrators reviewed her idea, thought it was good, and gave Laurie the names of some people she could talk to in order to get started. They also helped her put together a business plan. In return, Laurie had to create a report every month to let them know what she was doing to make her business grow.

Laurie Tandrup demonstrates her Butterfly Support car seat for newborns.

Like most Canadian inventors, Laurie applied for a patent in the United States first. The market is bigger in the U.S., and she knew that if she didn't have

Even with the success of her two inventions, Laurie still runs her business by herself out of the loft in her home. She can recognize the voice of each customer on the phone and likes it that way. Now she doesn't seek out new business—all of her customers learn about her products from other people who recommend them. She enjoys dealing with her regular customers and having time to spend with her two sons.

a U.S. patent, someone could copy her invention and make it a success there. She incorporated her company, just days before her product was to be featured in the Klondike Days Incredible Invention Forum, a fair in Edmonton. She called her company Snuglbuds Inc., after her nickname for Kaj, and she named her invention the Travelbud Support System.

Laurie had to work very hard to get ready for Klondike Days. It would have been too much work for her to make all the Travelbud cushions by herself, so she contracted out the sewing to a local company. Still, Laurie spent most nights staying up late cutting fabric and Velcro. Though Laurie's mother was an expert seamstress, Laurie did not share her love for the craft, and she couldn't wait to be finished. She was so overworked by all the preparations that she accidentally cut the tip of her thumb off! She went to the fair with stitches and a big bandage on her thumb—a testament to her dedication and hard work. Her efforts were worth it. The invention was a huge hit at Klondike Days, and she sold almost two hundred Travelbuds.

Now Laurie knew there was a demand for her product, but she still had to decide how and where to sell it. There were two problems with selling it in stores. First, it is very expensive to get a product sold in a big retail store. Secondly, if you sell something in a store that is not yours, there is no way to make sure that the person buying the product uses it properly. Since Laurie's invention was to be used on very small babies, it was very important to her that it be used in the right way. Many people do not use car seats correctly and Laurie knew that there was no way she could be sure that they would use the Travelbud the way that it was intended. Laurie's solution was to sell it directly to hospitals. When parents leave the hospital with their premature baby (a baby who is born early and who, in most cases, is very small and needs extra care) or a baby with special needs, the nurses or therapists spend some time with the parents to make sure they know how to position their baby so that they travel safely. Laurie knew that these special babies needed her Travelbud the most, so she felt hospitals were the best place to sell the product.

In 2001, Laurie began taking Kung Fu lessons with her oldest son, Kaj. Four years later, both were awarded their black belts. Laurie credits her positive attitude and sense of focus on the philosophy of the martial art. It has helped her in the challenges she has faced—like running her business while studying hard at school, and coping with an unexpected illness.

In the fall of 1996, Laurie went on a six-week road trip across Canada to visit hospitals and let them know about her Travelbud. From her old job as an operations manager at the hospital supply company, she knew some salespeople who could tell her whom she needed to talk to in the hospitals. Laurie had no sales experience, but she called the hospitals, made appointments, and came in to talk about and demonstrate her product. Word about her useful invention spread quickly. There was no similar product on the market. Laurie's Travelbud was unique because it was modular, which means that you could add pieces easily or take them away to adapt it to the baby's size, and it was affordable. Other products were custom-made, expensive, and did not adapt to the growing child.

Laurie's Travelbud was an immediate success, and as a bonus, she returned from her first trip with an idea for a second invention. When she visited the hospitals and talked with the therapists, she had realized that many people were trying to use the Travelbud to position infants in a way it had not originally been designed to do. One of her customers, Maureen Luther at the Women's College Hospital in Toronto, was the first to bring this specific positioning problem to her attention. After her visit with Maureen, Laurie soon found many people had the same problems, and she realized that another product was needed.

When a baby is born too early, before it has had time to develop its muscles enough to hold itself in a curled-up position, it will lie spread out on its back or belly. If this happens, its muscles don't develop properly. To prevent this problem, therapists try to get the baby back into the correct position. They had been trying to use the Travelbud to position these little babies.

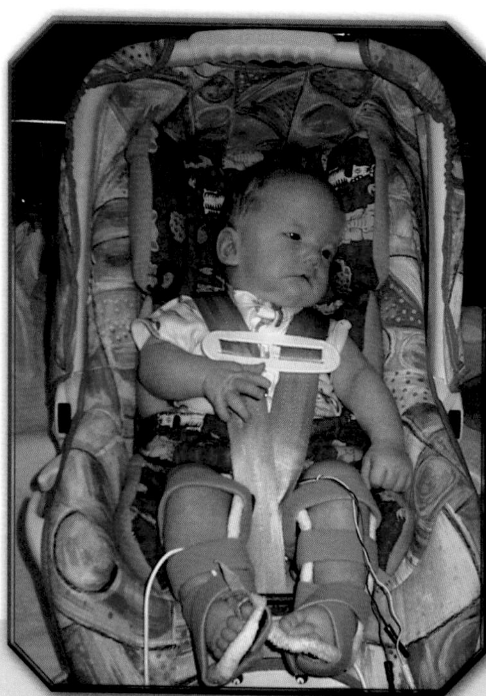

A young patient is ready to leave the hospital and drive home in style, thanks to Laurie Tandrup's Travelbud car seat.

When she got home, Laurie began work right away on her second invention, a new cushion that looked like a butterfly—and that's what she called it, Butterfly Support. She sent it to Maureen, who ordered more right away. Laurie didn't even have to make any changes because it was exactly what Maureen had wanted. Things began to move quickly, and Laurie filed for and received another patent for the Butterfly in 1997.

From the very beginning, it was clear that the Butterfly was a product for hospitals only. It allows the baby to lie in a range of positions, while at the same time keeping the infant pulled in and supported. Laurie's invention helps babies who have many different challenges—not just those who are born early.

When Laurie's sons started school, she began to volunteer in their classrooms. In 2001, she realized she wanted to be in a classroom full-time and decided to go back to school to become a teacher. She still ran her business while taking classes at Grant McEwan College and then the University of Alberta.

All seemed to be going well for Laurie. But things changed suddenly again in 2004. Laurie had been having problems hearing in class and went to the doctor to find out what was wrong. After some tests, she found out that she had an acoustic neuroma, which is a slow-growing tumor in her inner ear. Laurie was shocked, but dealt with the news the best way she could. Since her tumor was growing slowly, she chose to put off treatment, which could be quite difficult, until she was ready. She decided that she wanted to finish her degree first and take a trip with her sons before she had any treatment.

In 2006, Laurie reached her goal and graduated with a bachelor of education degree. For her summer vacation, she took her sons on a cross-country tour of Canada. They started in Edmonton and drove all the way to Newfoundland, where they met up with her husband for two weeks before turning around to drive home again. Since her business is small and she knows all of her customers well, Laurie was able to fill any orders before leaving. While traveling, she enjoyed the opportunity to stop by and say hello to many of her customers on her way across the country.

Her trip with the boys illustrates Laurie's spirit. No part of the trip was carefully planned. Instead they set off with a sense adventure, confident that they could handle whatever challenges they faced along the way, and ready to enjoy every moment of it. Life may have thrown Laurie many curves and set her on unexpected detours, but she has made the most of the ride.

Glossary

aeronautics The art and science of designing, making, and operating aircraft.

analyze To examine in detail in order to determine the nature or tendencies of something; to separate a thing or idea into its parts in order to discover their nature, proportion, function, or interrelationship.

aviation The art or science of flying airplanes; the development and operation of aircraft.

efficiency expert A person whose work is to increase the productive efficiency of a business or industry by finding better methods of performing various operations and reducing waste and costs.

engineering The science concerned with putting scientific knowledge to practical uses.

fission A splitting apart of the atom, dividing it into two parts.

frequency The number of periodic oscillations (fluctuations or variations), vibrations, or waves per unit of time, usually expressed in cycles per second.

inquisitive Inclined to ask many questions or seek information; eager to learn.

intellectual Possessing interests or tastes related to activities that involve or require the mind.

makeshift A thing that will do for a while as a substitute; a temporary measure, fix, or stand-in.

manufacturing The making of goods and articles, often on a large scale and with the help of machinery.

marketing All business activity involved in the moving of goods from the producer to the consumer, including selling, advertising, and packaging.

ophthalmology The branch of medicine dealing with the structure, functions, and diseases of the eye.

patent A document granting the monopoly right to produce, sell, or profit from an invention or process for a specific number of years; to secure exclusive right to produce, use, or sell an invention or process.

physics The science dealing with the properties, changes, and interactions of matter and energy, including electricity, heat, optics, mechanics, and atomic and nuclear energy.

prototype The first of its kind; the original; the model; the pattern; something that serves as a model for one of a later period.

radioactivity The state of giving off radiant energy in the form of particles or rays by the spontaneous disintegration of atomic nuclei.

segregation The policy or practice of compelling racial groups to live apart from each other, including the forced use of separate neighborhoods, schools, hotels, restaurants, churches, public transportation, and social facilities.

sharecropper Someone who works farmland in order to earn a share of the crop, the rest of which is paid to the landowner or landlord.

tonic A hair or scalp dressing, compound, cream, or lotion; anything that invigorates or stimulates, such as a drug or medicine.

For More Information

British Columbia Inventors Society
P.O. Box 43502
Alberni Street
Vancouver, BC V6G 3C7
Canada
(604) 779-4635
Web site: http://www.bcinventor.com

The BC Inventors Society is a registered nonprofit society. Its purposes are: to act as a forum for inventors to exchange ideas, information, and expertise; to encourage the success of new ideas or concepts in the marketplace; to provide collective support and business management skills for inventors whose new products are the source of industrial wealth; and to assist in the development of a vibrant provincial business economy and the creation of employment.

Canadian Intellectual Property Office (CIPO)
Place du Portage I
50 Victoria Street, Room C-114
Gatineau, QC K1A 0C9
Canada
(866) 997-1936
Web site: http://www.cipo.ic.gc.ca/eic/site/cipointernet-internetopic.nsf/eng/home

The Canadian Intellectual Property Office (CIPO) is responsible for the administration and processing of the greater part of intellectual property in Canada. CIPO's areas of activity include: patents, trademarks, copyrights, and industrial designs.

Invent Now Museum
221 South Broadway
Akron, OH 44308
(234) 678-6692
Web site: http://www.invent.org
The museum features 2,000 square feet of state-of-the-art multimedia and exhibits as well as a store featuring innovative products and themed apparel. Exhibits change annually and celebrate invention. The museum is free to the public.

Inventors' Alliance
P.O. Box 390219
Mountain View, CA 94039-390219
(650) 964-1576
Web site: http://www.inventorsalliance.org
The mission of the Inventors Alliance is to provide educational opportunities for inventors, with the goal of giving them the information they need to bring their products to market. The alliance supports independent inventors, product developers, and innovative companies through its educational and networking opportunities.

Inventors Assistance League, Inc. (AIL)
1053 Colorado Boulevard, Suite G1

Los Angeles, CA 90041
(877) IDEA-BIN (433-2246)
Web site: http://www.Inventions.org
The AIL seeks to take the mystery out of the patent, trademark, and copyright law, and to make it available to everyone in a manner that is easy to understand and easy to implement.

Inventors Digest
520 Elliot Street, Suite 200
Charlotte, NC 28202
(800) 838-8808
Web site: http://www.inventorsdigest.com
Inventors Digest is a magazine that fosters the spirit and practice of innovation and is committed to educating and inspiring independent and professional innovators. As the leading print and online publication for the innovation culture, *Inventors Digest* delivers useful, entertaining, and cutting-edge information to help its readers succeed.

National Inventors Hall of Fame and Museum
600 Dulany, Madison Building
Alexandria, VA 22314
(571) 272-0095
Web site: http://www.invent.org
The National Inventors Hall of Fame™ honors the women and men responsible for the great technological advances that make human, social, and economic progress possible. Each year, the Selection

Committee of the National Inventors Hall of Fame Foundation selects inventors for induction. These are selected from a field of people nominated by peers and the public. The Selection Committee includes representatives from the leading national scientific and technical organizations.

U.S. Patent and Trademark Office
P.O. Box 1450
Alexandria, VA 22313-1450
(800) 786-9199
Web site: http://www.uspto.gov
The United States Patent and Trademark Office (USPTO) is the federal agency for granting U.S. patents and registering trademarks. In doing this, the USPTO fulfills the mandate of Article I, Section 8, Clause 8, of the Constitution that the executive branch "promote the progress of science and the useful arts by securing for limited times to inventors the exclusive right to their respective discoveries." Under this system of protection, American industry has flourished. New products have been invented, new uses for old ones discovered, and employment opportunities created for millions of Americans. The strength and vitality of the U.S. economy depends directly on effective mechanisms that protect new ideas and investments in innovation and creativity. The USPTO advises the president of the United States, the secretary of commerce, and U.S. government agencies

on intellectual property (IP) policy, protection, and enforcement, and promotes the stronger and more effective IP protection around the world.

Web Sites

Due to the changing nature of Internet links, Rosen Publishing has developed an online list of Web sites related to the subject of this book. This site is updated regularly. Please use this link to access the list:

http://www.rosenlinks.com/gwoa/invnt

For Further Reading

Black Dog Publishing, ed. *Inventors and Inventions.* London, England: Black Dog Publishing, 2010.

Challoner, Jack. *1001 Inventions That Changed the World.* Hauppauge, NY: Barron's Educational Series, 2009.

Challoner, Jack. *Genius: Great Inventors and Their Creations.* London, England: Carlton Books, 2010.

Docie, Ronald Louis, Sr. *The Inventor's Bible: How to Market and License Your Brilliant Ideas.* 3rd ed. New York, NY: Ten Speed Press, 2010.

Foreman, Louis, and Jill Gilbert Welytok. *The Independent Inventor's Handbook: The Best Advice from Idea to Payoff.* New York, NY: Workman Publishing Company, Inc., 2009.

Gifford, Clive. *10 Inventors Who Changed the World.* New York, NY: Kingfisher, 2009.

Grissom, Fred, and David Pressman. *The Inventor's Notebook.* Berkeley, CA: NOLO, 2008.

Hamilton, Tyler. *Mad Like Tesla: Underdog Inventors and Their Relentless Pursuit of Clean Energy.* Toronto, ON: ECW Press, 2011.

Hobbs, John R. *The Secrets of Successful Inventors.* Sheffield, MA: Safe Goods, 2009.

Holmes, Keith C. *Black Inventors: Crafting Over 200 Years of Success.* Brooklyn, NY: Global Black Inventor Research Products, 2008.

Levy, Richard C. *The Complete Idiot's Guide to Cashing In on Your Inventions*. 2nd ed. New York, NY: Alpha, 2010.

Roberts, Dustyn. *Making Things Move: DIY Mechanisms for Inventors, Hobbyists, and Artists*. New York, NY: The McGraw-Hill Companies, 2011.

Spengler, Kremena. *An Illustrated Timeline of Inventions and Inventors*. Mankato, MN: Picture Window Books, 2011.

Sturm, Jeanne. *Inventors and Discoveries*. Vero Beach, FL: Rourke Publishing Group, 2011.

Sullivan, Otha Richard. *African American Inventors*. Hoboken, NJ: Wiley, 2011.

Wyckoff, Edwin. *Stopping Bullets with a Thread: Stephanie Kwolek and Her Incredible Invention*. Berkely Heights, NJ: Enslow Publishers, Inc., 2007.

Index

L

M

N

P

Q

S

T

W

About the Author

Sandra Braun is a writer and editor from Ottawa, Canada.

Photo Credits

Cover, pp. 1 (top), 87, 91, 93, 94 Myrna Maxwell/Courtesy Wendy Murphy; cover, pp. 1 (bottom), 49 Transcendental Graphics/Getty Images; pp. 9, 13 A'Lelia Bundles/Madam Walker Family Archives/madamcjwalker.com; p. 16 Library of Congress Prints and Photographs Division; p. 19 Central Press/Getty Images; p. 25 Keystone/Hulton Archive/Getty Images; pp. 29, 37, 38 (top), 57, 82 © AP Images; p. 34 Courtesy of Purdue University Libraries, Karnes Archives & Special Collections; p. 38 (bottom) Walter P. Reuther Library, Wayne State University; p. 39 Ashley & Crippen/Library and Archives Canada/PA-148464; p. 41 Library and Archives Canada/PA-200745; p. 45 Canada Aviation and Space Museum; p. 53 Hulton Archive/Getty Images; p. 65 © DuPont; p. 69 U.S. Marine Corps/DefenseImagery.Mil; p. 71 krtillustrationslive007144/Newscom; p. 76 Shutterstock; p. 77 spnphotostwo285023/Newscom; p. 80 http://en.wikipedia.org/wiki/File:Founders_Library,_Howard_University.jpg; p. 85 USPTO; pp. 95, 98, 99, 102 Courtesy Laurie Tandrup; multiple interior graphics © www.istockphoto.com/henrikroger.